MANY LONG YEARS AGO

OGDEN NASH

MANY LONG YEARS AGO

LONDON: J. M. DENT & SONS LTD

PUBLISHERS' NOTE

This volume has been compiled from Ogden Nash's earlier works, which were published in America but not in this country. The poems, which will be new to British readers, have been arranged afresh and revised by the author for the British edition.

The publication of this collection, taken together with the reissue of The Face is Familiar and the other later volumes already in print, namely Good Intentions, Versus, Family Reunion, and The Private Dining-Room, now makes available in this country the entire body of verse which the author wishes to preserve in book form.

London, 1954.

CONTENTS

vii

AWAY FROM IT ALL

I wish I were a Tibetan monk
Living in a monastery.
I would unpack my trunk
And store it in a tronastery;
I would collect all my junk
And send it to a jonastery;
I would try to reform a drunk,
And pay his expenses at a dronastery.
If my income shrunk
I would send it to a shronastery.

Fish are very good at swimming,
And the ocean with them is brimming.
They stay under water all year round,
And they never get drowned,
And they have a gift more precious than gold,
Which is that they never catch cold.
No, they may not be as tasty as venison or mooseflesh,
But they never get gooseflesh.
They have been in the ocean since they were roe,
So they don't have to creep into it toe by toe,
And also they stay in it permanently, which must be a
    source of great satisfaction,
Because they don't have to run dripping and shivering up
    and down the beach waiting vainly for a healthy
    reaction.
Indeed when I think how uncomplicated the ocean is for
    fish my thoughts grow jealous and scathing,
Because when fish bump into another fish it doesn't wring
    from them a cry of Faugh! and ruin their day's bathing.
No, if it's a bigger fish than they are, they turn round and
    beat it,
And if it's littler, they eat it.
Some fish are striped and some are speckled,
But none of them ever heard of ultra-violet rays and felt it
    necessary to lie around getting sand in their eyes and
    freckled.
Oh, would it not be wondrous to be a fish? No, it
    would not be wondrous,
Because we unmarine humans are at the top of the animal
    kingdom and it would be very undignified to change
    places with anything under us.

THE LIFE OF THE PARTY

Lily, there isn't a thing you lack,
Your effect is simply stunning.
But Lily, your gown is low in the back,
So conduct yourself with cunning.
Some of your charm is charm of face,
But some of your charm is spinal;
Losing your looks is no disgrace,
But losing your poise is final.
Ridicule's name is Legion,
So look to your dorsal region.

For Bartie,
Old Bartie,
The life of the party,
Is practically perfect tonight;
He's prettily, properly tight;
He's never appeared so bright.
Have you ever seen Bartie
Enliven a party?
You've never seen Bartie—
Why, Lord love a duck!
At present old Bartie is running amok.
There's a wink in his eye
And a smile on his lips
For the hostess he tickles,
The butler he trips.
There's a rubber cigar,
And a smoking-room jest,
To melt the reserve
Of the clerical guest.
There's a pin for the man who stoops over,
And a little trained flea for Rover.
So Lily, beware of your back!
More daring than duller and older blades,
Bartie is hot on the track.

I've noticed him eyeing your shoulder blades.
And maybe it's salad,
And maybe it's ice,
But I fear he has planned
Some amusing device,
For the laughter is slack
And he's taking it hard—
He's eyeing your back—
And Bartie's a card—
He's forming a plan—
May I fetch you a shawl?—
That inventive young man—
There is one in the hall.
Though your back is divine
In its natural state,
May I curtain your spine?—
Dear Heaven, I'm late!
Aren't you glad that you came to the party?
And weren't you amused by Bartie?

Horace, the moment that you appeared,
I admired your manly beauty,
But I feel that a word about your beard
Is only my honest duty.
Your tailor's craft is a gentleman's dream,
Your suavity leaves me lyrical,
But escaping tonight with your self-esteem
Will require a minor miracle.
Fun is a gay deceiver,
So look to your kingly beaver.

For Bartie,
Old Bartie,
The life of the party,
Is cutting it wide to-night.
No bushel obscures his light.
He's knocking them left and right.

4

Have you ever seen Bartie
Enliven a party?
You've never seen Bartie—
My lad, you're in luck,
For Bartie, old Bartie, is running amok.
At Bartie's approach
Lesser wags droop.
Have you seen the tin roach
He drops in your soup?
Is a spoon in your pocket?
Or gum in your chair?
It's Bartie, old Bartie,
Who magicked them there.
And of those who complain, there's a rumour
That they're lacking a sense of humour.
So Horace, beware of your beard!
I scent some fantastic flubdubbery!
Old Bartie has just disappeared
And I've noticed him eyeing your shrubbery.
And maybe it's syrup,
And maybe it's mice,
But I fear he has planned
Some amusing device.
His conceptions are weird,
And nothing is barred—
He was eyeing your beard—
And Bartie's a card—
When Bartie returns,
The fun will begin—
May I fetch you a bag
To put on your chin?
Just a small paper bag
To envelop the bait?—
For Bartie's a wag—
Dear Heaven, I'm late!
Aren't you glad that you came to the party?
And weren't you amused by Bartie?

There are several generally recognized grounds for divorce,
And there are moments when stealing is a starving man's
  only recourse;
There are gatherings when it is perfectly proper to tell a
  dubious story if there is sufficient wit in it,
And there are provocations under which it is allowable
  to pull away an old lady's chair as she is about to sit
  in it,
But there is one unpardonable sin and in extenuation of
  it let us quote no Ballads of Reading Gaol and in
  praise of it let us chant no merry madrigals,
And that is amateur theadrigals.
Now, the urge to dress up and pretend to be somebody
  else is a universal human weakness,
Like never going to church except on Easter and then
  crowding out all the people who have been there the
  other fifty-one Sundays of the year, or never going to
  the races except for the Belmont or the Preakness.
So if some alternate All-Eastern left tackle who has been
  told he looks like Noel Coward wants to toss badinage
  back and forth like a medicine ball with a Junior
  Leaguer who has been told that with her glasses off
  she looks like Gertrude Lawrence,
Why that's their business, like drinking sidecars in bed
  or putting maple walnut ice cream on their oysters,
  and if they kept it to themselves it could be viewed
  with tolerance as well as abhorrence,
But the trouble is that they refuse to indulge their depraved
  appetites in the privacy of deserts or cloisters,
The kick is missing unless a lot of people are on hand to
  watch them drink sidecars in bed or put maple walnut
  ice cream on their oysters,
So they inveigle all their friends and relatives and all the
  relatives of their friends and all the friends of their
  relatives, in the name of various worthy charities,

Into paying for the privilege of sitting for three hours on piano stools and watching them project their personalities across the footlights with the gusto and *élan* of Oriental beggars exhibiting their physical peculiarities.

Tonight I am being taken to see the Troubadour Players do *The Merchant of Venice*.

I shall go with the same eagerness with which, if I weren't me, I should pay three dollars to watch me play tennis.

Breakfast is an institution that I don't know who com-
    menced it,
But I am not for it, I am against it.
It is a thoroughly inedible repast,
And the dictionary says it is derived from the words
    break, meaning to break, and fast, meaning a fast, so
    to breakfast means to break your fast.
Well that just shows how far you can trust a dictionary,
Because I never saw a definition that was more utterly
    fictionary.
The veriest child could see it doesn't check,
Because if the first syllable of breakfast means to break,
    why is it pronounced brek?
Shame on you, you old lexicographers, I shall call you
    laxicographers because you have grown very lax,
Because it is perfectly obvious that the first syllable in
    breakfast is derived from the far-famed Yale football
    cheer, which is Brekekekex co-ax co-ax,
And did you even get the second syllable right? Why a
    thousand times No,
Because the fast in breakfast doesn't mean fast, abstinence
    from food, it means fast, not slow.
So with that in mind we can peek behind the scenes
And then we can see what break-fast really means,
It means that if you wake up in the morning feeling un-
    appetized and sickly,
Why you are confronted by a meal and the entire Yale
    football team coaxes you with an axe to eat it quickly.
On this topic I could write a chapter,
But I will content myself with saying that the French
    word for breakfast, which is déjeuner, is considerably
    apter,
Because it is perfectly truthful,
Because it is made up of the words de, meaning to un-
    something, and jeuner, which must be derived from

8

the word *jeune*, meaning young, so *jeuner* must mean
to grow youthful,
So I think that is the reason that the French are always
bright and gay,
Because they never eat breakfast because they are warned
off it by their word for it, which means something
that if you eat it you will grow unyouthful right away.

St Valentine's day is a February day,
St Patrick's falls in March;
St Swithin's day votes yea or nay
On whether we drip or parch.
St Patrick trod the Irish sod,
By choice, if not by birth,
And I'm unaware of exactly where
St Swithin walked the earth.
But Valentine, St Valentine,
I trust he trod on a porcupine.

The snakes and ladders of his day
Was a game that was played by Patrick;
An efficient saint in his chosen way,
Though perhaps a mite theatric.
St Swithin did I know not what,
But piecing the bits together,
I suppose his claim to immortal fame
Had something to do with weather.
But Valentine became the patron
Of the maid who'd rather be a matron.

St Patrick's day is brave and bold,
With the music blaring gaily,
With buckles and braid and a big parade,
And shamrock and shillelagh.
St Swithin's day is a splendid day
And I'm glad that the day is his,
Though every year, I regret to say,
I forget which day it is.
But Valentine, St Valentine,
His day is over-endocrine.

St Valentine's day is a spooner's day,
A day of reeking loves,
When they stuff the marts with bleeding hearts
And pestiferous twittering doves.

O crooner's day, O swooner's day,
O day of versicles vile,
O day of the smile in every tear,
And the tear in every smile!
Marshmallow whip and mailing lists!
Meringue of exhibitionists!

Then be my angel, dearest dear,
My darling and my poppet,
My gambolling lamb, my ham what am,
My priceless Persian carpet.
Be my gazelle, my wishing well,
My sacred garden spot,
My *raison d'être*, etc., etc.,
But never my you-knew-what.
Be everything, my love, that's mine.
But not if I know it, my Valentine.

Once there was a girl named Miriam,
And she spent part of her time in a delirium,
And she said, I wish the world were a little less mysterious,
Because I do like to know when I am delirious,
But I have discovered that whenever I regard the world
and judge it logical and normal and headed for the
millennium at a mile a minute,
Why that's the time I ought to be enclosed in a spacious
park with an asylum in it,
But whenever everybody else seems to be running around
in a delirium,
Why that's the time when somebody may be fuzzy-
minded, but it isn't Miriam.
So finally she convened an enormous convention, national
and international,
And she said, Please I wish everybody would help me to
determine when I am delirious and when I am rational,
Because, she said, at present I am just a bit hazy,
Because when I am crazy you all seem perfectly sane, but
when I am sane you all seem perfectly crazy,
So, she said, forgive me if I am too personal or informal,
But I hope from now on you will all behave so that I will
think you are delirious if I am delirious, and normal if
I am normal,
So they all said, What a good idea, hurrah for Miriam!
Who are we? Who are we? We are the boys and girls
of the Eastern and Western hemispheres, and we are
going to help her with her delirium!
So from then on manias were declared reprehensible,
And everybody tried to be sensible,
And there wasn't any more war,
And there were only as many people dancing at night
clubs as could comfortably get on the floor,
And all the rich people cried Soak the rich, and all the poor
people cried No that would retard recovery, soak the poor!

And the tailors made men's and women's coats with the buttons on the same side, and that stopped a lot of argument between husbands and wives as to the comparative intelligence of men and women, you may be sure.

And what with one thing and another everybody was sensible and lived happily ever after and they said they owed it all to Miriam,

So they offered her the dictatorship of the world, but she never used it, only in a delirium.

DRAGONS ARE TOO SELDOM

To actually see an actual marine monster
Is one of the things that do before I die I wonster.
Should you ask me if I desire to meet the bashful in-
    habitant of Loch Ness,
I could only say yes.
Often my eye with moisture dims
When I think that it has never been my good fortune
    to gaze on one of Nature's whims.
Far from ever having seen a Gorgon
I haven't even seen the midget that sat in the lap of Mr
    J. Pierpont Morgan.
Indeed it is my further ill fortune or mishap
That far from having seen the midget that sat in it I have
    never even seen Mr J. Pierpont Morgan's lap.
Indeed I never much thought about Mr J. Pierpont Mor-
    gan's having a lap because just the way you go into
    churches and notice the stained glass more than the
    apses
When you think about multi-millionaires you don't
    think about their laps as much as their lapses;
But it seems that they do have laps which is one human
    touch that brings them a little closer to me and you,
And maybe they even go so far as to sometimes have
    hiccups too.
But regular monsters like sea serpents don't have laps or
    hiccups or any other characteristic that is human,
And I would rather see a second-rate monster such as a
    mermaid than a first-rate genius such as John Bunyan
    or Schiaparelli or Schubert or Schumann;
Yes, I would rather see one of the sirens
Than two Lord Byrons,
And if I knew that when I got there I could see Cyclops
    or Scylla and Charybdis or Pegasus
I would willingly walk on my hands from here to Dallas,
    Tegasus,

14

Because I don't mean to be satirical,
But where there's a monster there's a miracle,
And after a thorough study of current affairs, I have
   concluded with regret
That the world can profitably use all the miracles it can get,
And I think life would be a lot less demoralizing,
If instead of sitting around in front of the radio listening
   to torture singers sing torture songs we sat around
   listening to the Lorelei loreleising.

There was a poet who asked out loud,
'O why should the spirit of mortal be proud?'
The which is a typical poet's question
Born of temper or indigestion,
For poets, when their affairs go wrong,
Take it out in satiric song;
If all on their own they fall from grace,
They blast the whole of the human race;
They resent, when mocked by a passport photo,
Not their face, but mankind in toto.
Poets believe in pixies and elves
And blaming everyone but themselves.
Such was the poet who asked out loud
'O why should the spirit of mortal be proud?'
A notable piece of rhymed invective,
Which proves the poet had no perspective.
His argument wins for the other side;
For the spirit of mortal should swell with pride
At producing the poet who asked out loud
'O why should the spirit of mortal be proud?'
The more annoyed that a poet gets,
The deeper he's buried in duns and debts,
The more he's flouted and jeered and jilted,
The further his cup of woe is tilted,
The more his liver is misbehaving,
The more that he cuts himself while shaving,
The further his collar buttons roll,
The blacker the clouds that shadow his soul,
Why, the greater his scorn for his fellow man,
And a wasp is what he is busier than;
Apoplexy he's on the brink of,
He writes the nastiest he can think of.
Yet the more that the world by him is scorned,
The more is the world by him adorned,
And the more at mortals he bites his thumbs,

The more immortal he becomes,
For people share through all creation
One weakness of the American nation;
The books they prize upon their shelves
Say the horridest things about themselves.
Is this fact hidden from the poet,
Or does the unscrupulous scribbler know it?

THE JAPANESE

How courteous is the Japanese;
He always says, 'Excuse it, please.'
He climbs into his neighbour's garden,
And smiles, and says, 'I beg your pardon';
He bows and grins a friendly grin,
And calls his hungry family in;
He grins, and bows a friendly bow;
'So sorry, this my garden now.'

17

FRIEND OF MY FRIEND

Every schoolboy is taught by his teacher, if not by his
　　mother,
That things which are equal to the same thing are equal
　　to each other,
But that is a lesson of which every schoolboy should be
　　an eschewer,
Because almost nothing could be untruer,
Because even if it is partly true there is one point where
　　its veracity ends,
And that is the point of your friends.
Now we can assume without any fuss
That all our friends are equal to us,
And we do not have to haw and hem
In stating that we are equal to all of them,
So therefore according to our teacher or our mother,
All our friends are equal to the same thing, which is us,
　　so they ought to be equal to each other,
But it is my complaint
That they ain't.
You have two favourite friends and you introduce them
　　to each other and you think it is going to be a big
　　treat, but no treat could be littler,
Because the meeting is about as genial as a meeting of
　　Rabbi Wise and Hitler,
And disapproval is rampant,
And your enthusiasm for introducing your friends to
　　each other is dampent,
But these meetings aren't over when they are through,
No, because all your friends go around blaming all your
　　other friends on you,
And the way it ends
Is that not only do your friends fail to fraternize, but they
　　stop being friends with you, because they can't stand
　　your friends,

So if you have a couple of friends who are very close to
  your heart,
For heaven's sake keep them apart,
Because otherwise I take my oath
You're going to lose 'em both.

FROM A MANHATTAN TOMB

I know that a little verse is a versicle but I don't know if a
little phrase is a phrasicle

But I do know that at the moment I feel too too alas and
alackadaisicle.

What though around me is the hustle and bustle of a great
city at its labours?

What though I am hemmed in by the most industrious
and ingenious kind of neighbours?

What though young people are joining forever or part-
ing forever with each tick of the clock?

What though Mr Belloc admires Mr Chesterton or Mr
Chesterton admires Mr Belloc?

What though to produce the Sunday papers thousands of
square miles of Canada are deforested?

What though in an attempt to amuse the public thousands of writers and actors and things are utterly
exhorested?

What though young humans are getting born and old
humans are getting deceased and middle-aged humans
are getting used to it?

What though a Bronxville husband has discovered that he
can put the baby to sleep by reading Proust to it?

All these things may be of great moment to those who
are concerned with them in any way,

But how are they going to help me to get through the
day?

For I have had to eat luncheon while I was still sorry I
had eaten breakfast and I shall have to eat dinner while
I am still sorry I ate luncheon

And my spirit has been put through the third degree and
thrown into a very dark dank dismal duncheon.

Why do people insist on bringing me anecdotes and
allegories and alcohol and food?

Why won't they just let me sit and brood?

Why does the population swirl around me with vivacious
  violence
When all I want to do is sit and suffer in siolence?
Everybody I see tries to cheer me up
And I wish they would stop.

A WARNING TO FIANCÉES

The golfer is as strange a beast
As ever roamed the earth;
On daily sorrow doth he feast,
And ghastly is his mirth.

A human form the golfer owns,
And eke a human face;
To outward sight like Smith or Jones,
One of the human race.

Yet his is not the blood that's in
The veins of Jones and Smith;
The lesser apes are nearer kin,
The clouds are closer kith.

With sunken head and feet that lag,
The golfer prowls apart;
With sevens lurking in his bag
And birdies in his heart.

Sometimes he beats the sand alone,
A figure lorn and gruesome;
Sometimes he mingles with his own
In foursome or in twosome.

His laws are not the laws of men;
Indeed, he seems to thrive
On holing out in nine or ten
And scoring it as five.

Yet if by chance he make a four,
He leapeth not in glee,
But proveth with detail galore
It should have been a three.

For ever doth the golfer roam;
Odysseus might have been one;
Perhaps the golfer has a home,
But I've never seen one in one.

So, bridesmaids, weep for the golfer's wife,
And shun her dreary fate,
For the lighthouse keeper sees more life
Than the golfer's lonely mate.

Oh, sometimes I sit around and think, what would you do
    if you were up a dark alley and there was Caesar Borgia,
And he was coming torgia,
And brandished a poisoned poniard,
And looked at you like an angry fox looking at the plump-
    est rooster in a boniard?
Why that certainly would be an adventure,
It would be much more exciting than writing a poem or
    selling a debenture,
But would you be fascinated,
Or just afraid of being assassinated?
Or suppose you went out dancing some place where you
    generally dance a lot,
And you jostled somebody accidentally and it turned out
    to be Sir Lancelot,
And he drew his sword,
Would you say Have at you! or would you say Oh Lord!?
Or what if you were held up by a bandit,
And he told you to hand over your money, would you try
    to disarm him and turn him over to the police, or would
    you over just meekly hand it?
What would you do if you were in a luxurious cosmopoli-
    tan hotel surrounded by Europeans and Frenchmen,
And a beautiful woman came up to you and asked you to
    rescue her from some mysterious master mind and his
    sinister henchmen?
Would you chivalrously make her rescue your personal
    objective,
Or would you refer her to the house detective?
Yes, and what if you were on trial for murdering some-
    body whom for the sake of argument we might call
    Kelly or O'Connor,
And you were innocent but were bound to be convicted
    unless you told the truth and the truth would tarnish a
    lady's honour,

Would you elect to die like a gentleman or live like a
poltroon,
Or put the whole thing in the hands of an arbitration
committee headed by Heywood Broun?
Yes, often as through life I wander
This is the kind of question I ponder,
And what puzzles me most is why I even bother to ponder
when I already know the answer,
Because anybody who won't cross the street till the lights
are green would never get far as a Musketeer or a Bengal
Lancer.

HYMN TO THE SUN AND MYSELF

Well! Well!
The day's at the morn!
Dandy old day!
Dandy old morn!
Oh! Look!
The hillside's dew-pearled!
Nicely old hillside!
Nicely dew-pearled!
And oh! Look!
The snail's on the thorn!
Lucky old snail!
Lucky old thorn!
Well! Well!
All's right with the world!
Hurrah for the right!
Hurrah for the world!

For oh! what a day it is today, my lads!
Oh! my lads, what a day it is today!
At 11.07 a.m. I'll be 27¾ years old,
An age dear to me because it was once passed through
  by Edna St Vincent Millay.
Oh what fun to be young and healthy and alive
And privileged to do some of the work of the world
  from nine to five!
Oh let me be truly thankful for every one of those 27¾
  years;
For not having been run over by the Lexington Avenue
  Express or gored by runaway steers;
For not having been able to afford a passage on the
  Titanic,
And for not having had any money to lose in the recent
  stock market panic;
For never having written a best-seller, only to be wounded
  by the critics;

For never having gotten impeached for making millions
in dirty politics;
For never having made any enemies by getting ahead too
speedily;
For not finding the world at my feet while still as young
as Lindbergh or Gertrude Ederle;
For not having tried to impress my girl but being naturaler
with her and naturaler;
So that now instead of having to marry and all that I can
continue to be a careless baturaler;
Above all let me be thankful for something rarer than
gold—
Viz.: that at 11.07 a.m. I'll be $27\frac{3}{4}$ years old.
Oh let my future be as lucky as my past!
Oh let every day for a long time not be my last!

Sometimes it's difficult, isn't it, not to grow grim and
    rancorous
Because man's fate is so counter-clockwise and can-
    tankerous.
Look at all the noble projects that die a-borning,
Look how hard it is to get to sleep at night and then how
    hard it is to wake up in the morning!
Look how when people look at a girl in cold blood they
    can see that she is bow-legged or cross-eyed or thinks
    she is so wonderful or nags or chatters,
And then look how they don't notice it at all when they
    are in love with her which is the critical time when it
    really matters.
How easy to be unselfish in the big things that never come
    up and how hard in the little things that come up daily
    and hourly, oh yes,
Such as what heroic pleasure to give up the last seat in a
    lifeboat to a mother and babe, and what an irritation
    to give some dowdy housewife your seat on the Lexing-
    ton Avenue Express!
How easy for those who do not bulge
To not overindulge!
O universe perverse, why and whence your perverseness?
Why do you not teem with betterness instead of worseness?
Why is it your gospel
To go around making everything just as complicated as
    pospel?
Do you get your only enjoyment
Out of humanity's annoyment?
Because a point I would like to discuss
Is, why wouldn't it be just as easy for *you* to make things
    easy for us?
But no, you will not listen, expostulation is useless,
Home is the fisherman empty-handed, home is the hunter
    caribouless and mooseless.

Humanity must continue to follow the sun around
And accept the eternal run-around.
Well, if that be the case, why come on humanity!
So long as it is our fate to be irked all our life let us just
keep our heads up and take our irking with insouciant
urbanity.

HARK! HARK! THE PARI-MUTUELS BARK!

I

Willow waley and woe and sorrow,
The horses are coming to town tomorrow.
Chestnut and bay and black and grey
Sport and cavort and snort and neigh.
The horses, the horses are on the way!
The horses are coming to town tomorrow,
And some must beg and others borrow.
The horses are coming, enter the horses,
Exit the remnant of my resources,
Here goes me, and never a doubt of it,
And the horses don't even get anything out of it.
They don't get money or love or fun,
Why in the world must the horses run?
Or if they must, through a fate unholy,
Why must some of them run so slowly?
Brothers, the country's crying need
Is horses that run at an equal speed
And a stone-dead heat on every track
And everyone getting their money back.
Willow waley and woe and sorrow,
The horses are coming to town tomorrow.
Every horse with a personal grudge
Against this modestly hopeful judge,
Holding its life as cheap as a song
If its death in the stretch should prove me wrong.
Well listen horses, I know you hate me,
But do not think to intimidate me.
Or drive from the track, by deed or threat,
The man who has never cashed a bet.
One day I shall hold a winning ticket,
And swagger up to the teller's wicket,

And take my money and catch a boat
To the land of the horsemeat table d'hôte.
Oh, I'll sit in Paris till Doomsday breaks
Chewing over my old mistakes.

II

O, racing is a ruinous sport,
The race track is an ill resort,
My waxing poverty I owe to it,
I often wonder why I go to it;
I hate the horses I have bet on,
I hate the horses my heart is set on;
Some are outsiders, some are sure things,
But if mine own, are ever poor things.
I hate the hunches, I hate the dope,
I hate the fear, I hate the hope,
I hate the blinkers, I hate the wrappers,
I hate the trainers and handicappers,
I hate the dust, I hate the mud,
I hate the pulsation of sporting blood,
I hate the jumps, I hate the flat,
And the red-hot tips from the stable cat,
The silly saddles, the foolish stirrups,
And the hang-arounders' cheerful chirrups,
The inhuman machines and human bookies,
And the plungers with faces like man-eating cookies,
The rattle and drum of the pounding hoof,
The triumphant shout that rocks the roof.
I hate my horse to be out in front
Lest he should wilt beneath the brunt;
I hate to see my horse behind,
Lest he be trapped in a pocket blind,
And when my horse is in the centre,
The hooks I hang upon are tenter,
And oh, the microphones that retch
And tell you who's leading in the stretch!

Into your helpless ear they quack
Who's moving up, who's falling back,
Your fingers would find their gullets, if
From tearing up tickets they weren't so stiff.
I mean it when I feelingly state
That racing is my bitterest hate.
But of all emotions within the breast,
Hate is by far the ugli-est.
To ugly hate I will not yield,
But bet five dollars on the field.

I WANT TO SIT NEXT TO EMILY

I know a girl who for present purposes let us call by the
name of Emily,
And let me state at once that she is not a member of my
immediate or unimmediate family;
Neither is her habitat
The city or state where I keep my bed and board and faith-
ful dog and talkative parrot and celibate white rabbit at;
I simply say that she lives not as near as the next street and
not as far away as Samoa,
And I knoa.
I am told that her conversation doesn't appeal to the in-
tellectual or arty,
But I must confess that I enjoy sitting next to Emily at a party.
She always refers to Colonel Charles A. Lindbergh as
Lucky Lindy and to his flight as a hop,
And she says that once she starts eating pretzels and potato
chips she can never stop;
She is quick to size up a situation, for I have often heard her aver
That she likes lobster but lobster doesn't like her.
She believes that every boy should go to college not so
much for the sake of learning higher mathematics and
physics and beautiful poems like Hiawatha and The Last
Ride from Ghent to Aix,
But particularly because of the useful social contacts that
he makes.
She calls the Notre Dames the Fighting Irish despite their
individual rather un-Hibernian nomenclature,
And believes that football is an invaluable character-
builder and war is certainly hell all right but what's
the use of trying to do anything about it because you
can't abolish war until you abolish human nature.
She says she is broadminded enough to admire Mencken's
jokes and witticisms,
But she wishes he would realize that what this country needs
is fewer DEstructive and more CONstructive criticisms.

She says she has her own opinions about Eugene O'Neill but
    she doesn't want necessarily to fight about them,
But at the same time real life is so full of unpleasant things
    that she doesn't see why people have to go and write
    about them.
She likes to visit New York, but how New Yorkers live
    the life they live day in and day out she doesn't know,
    she is sure,
And she rather sadly says that after all the French are the
    only people who know anything about l'amour.
She admits that she has often been covered with confusion
    and shame
Because though she can never forget a face she can never
    remember a name.
She has a new bon mot of which she is very proud;
She wants to know if you have heard that N.R.A. means
    No Republicans Allowed.
She says she hasn't told it very well, but when George
    told it to her it was exquisite,
Because George has a gift that way and when all is said and
    done it's not so much what you say as how you say it,
    is it?
Dear Emily, let others make horrid remarks about your
    conversation;
To me in an unrelaxed world it is a haven of relaxation.
Seated beside you, my dear my darling Emily, I can be
    perfectly polite murmuring yes yes and no no and don't
    have to fret myself thinking up brilliant and penetrating
    retorts,
But can wander lonely as a cloud among my own beautiful
    thorts.

HELPFUL REFLECTION

A good way to forget today's sorrows
Is by thinking hard about tomorrow's.

I'M TERRIBLY SORRY FOR YOU, BUT I CAN'T HELP LAUGHING

Everybody has a perfect right to do what they please,
But one thing that I advise everybody not to do is to contract a laughable disease.
There is something impressive about cholera,
And anybody who undergoes an operation gets a reputation for courage even if they are a screaming cowardly hollera;
People speak of you respectfully if you catch bubonic,
And if you get typhus they think you have done something positively mastodonic;
One touch of leprosy makes the whole world your kin,
And even a slight concussion earns you an anxious inquiry and not a leering grin.
Yes, as long as people are pretty sure you have something you are going to be removed by,
Why they are very sympathetic, and books and flowers and visits and letters are what their sympathy is proved by.
But unfortunately there are other afflictions anatomical,
And people insist on thinking that a lot of them are comical,
And if you are afflicted with this kind of affliction people are amused and disdainful,
Because they are not bright enough to realize that an affliction can be ludicrous and still be ominous and painful.
Suppose for instance you have a dreadful attack of jaundice, what do they do?
They come around and smile and say Well well, how are you today, Dr Fu-Manchu?
The early martyrs thought they knew what it was to be taken over the jumps,
But no martyr really ought to get his diploma until he has undergone his friends' witticisms during his mumps.

When you have laryngitis they rejoice,
Because apparently the funniest thing in the world is
when you can't curse and swear at them for laughing at
your lost voice, because you have lost your voice.
Toothache is another diversion that hearty amusement
yields,
And if you have a severe enough case of sunburn they
find you funnier than W. C. Fields.
And as for boils,
Well, my pen recoils,
Because people's invariable humorous remarks about
other people's boils are invariably unprintable,
And most of them are not even hintable.
So I advise you, at the risk of being pedantic,
If you must be sick, by all means choose a sickness that
is preferably fatal and certainly romantic,
Because it is much better to have that kind of sickness
and be sick unto death or anyway half to death,
Than to have the other kind and be laughed to death.

MAE WEST

Westward the course of vampire moves its way;
The concave bosom sinks into eclipse;
Everywhere happy endings flatter Mae,
And ape the pace that launched a thousand hips.

MR BARCALOW'S BREAKDOWN

Once there was a man, and he was named Mr Barcalow,
to be exact,
And he prided himself on his tact,
And he said, One thing about an apple, it may have a
worm in it, and one thing about a chimney, it may
have soot in it,
But one thing about my mouth, I never put my foot in it.
Now never was Mr Barcalow's tact so exquisite
As when he went for a visit,
Because whenever he entered a community
He inquired of his host and hostess what topics he could
discuss with impunity,
So no matter beside whom he was deposited,
Why, he could talk to them without disturbing any
skeletons that should have been kept closeted,
But one dire day he went to visit some friends,
And he started asking tactful questions about untactful
conversational trends,
And his host said that here was one place that Mr Barcalow
wouldn't need his tact,
Because taboos and skeletons were what everybody there
lacked,
And his hostess said, That's right, but you'd better not
mention bathrooms to Emily, who you will sit by at
lunch,
Because her grandmother was scalded to death in a shower
shortly after complaining that there was no kick in the
punch,
And his host said, Oh yes, and steer away from edu-
cation when you talk to the Senator,
Because somebody said his seventeen-year-old nephew
would have to burn down the schoolhouse to get out
of the third grade and his nephew overheard them and
did burn down the schoolhouse, including the music
teacher and the janitor,

And his hostess said, Oh yes, and if you talk about love and marriage to Mrs Musker don't be surprised if her eye sort of wanders,

Because her daughter is the one who had the divorce suit with thirty-seven co-responders,

And his host said, Oh yes, and you'd better know that the war is Florence's mania,

Because her cousin-in-law was the man who sank the Lusitania,

And Mr Barcalow said, Well, can I talk about sports,

And his hostess said, Well maybe you'd better not because Louise's sister, the queer one, was asked to resign from the club because she went out to play moonlight tennis in shorts, and Mr Barcalow said That's not so terrible is it, everybody wears shorts, and his hostess said, Yes, but she forgot the shorts,

So Mr Barcalow said, Well then, what about the Weather,

And his host said Well, that's what we used to discuss when we got together,

But it has recently become a pleasure we must defer,

Because Jane's Aunt Julia is here from California and she seems to think every remark about the weather is a personal affront to her.

So Mr Barcalow said, The hell with you all, and went upstairs and packed,

And that was the last that was ever heard of Mr Barcalow and his tact.

A BAS BEN ADHEM

My fellow man I do not care for
I often ask me, What's he there for?
The only answer I can find
Is, Reproduction of his kind.
If I'm supposed to swallow that,
Winnetka is my habitat.
Isn't it time to carve Hic Jacet
Above that Reproduction racket?

To make the matter more succinct:
Suppose my fellow man extinct.
Why, who would not approve the plan
Save possibly my fellow man?
Yet with a politician's voice
He names himself as Nature's choice.

The finest of the human race
Are bad in figure, worse in face.
Yet just because they have two legs
And eat, instead of laying, eggs,
They count the spacious firmament
As something to be charged and sent.

Though man created cross-town traffic,
The Daily Mirror, News, and Graphic,
The pastoral fight and fighting pastor,
And Queen Marie and Lady Astor,
He hails himself with drum and fife
And bullies lower forms of life.

Not that I think that much depends
On how we treat our feathered friends,
Or hold the wrinkled elephant
A nobler creature than my aunt.
It's simply that I'm sure I can
Get on without my fellow man.

They are constantly getting themselves bedizened,
And they say it is you they are doing it for, but it isn't.
Oh no, dear fellow male, it has nothing whatsoever to do
With either me or you,
Because if it was only a question of doing it for us,
The bedizening would require fewer feathers and much
less fuss.
Oh yes, they say they bedeck themselves to make them-
selves attractive to their mate, potential or actual,
But I am afraid that that statement of theirs is not factual,
Because if there is one thing about which they are not
reverential,
It is any opinion of their clothes expressed by their mate,
actual or potential,
And any mate venturing to express any such opinion
Soon finds himself less than a minion,
And this is a statement which can really be put to the
touch,
Because just remember the last time that yours wore
something that you admired specially much,
And you had a lot of enthusiastic praise and were not
sparing of it,
And said Oh what a lovely dress, and hoped there would
be frequent wearing of it,
Because it was a dress of which you were very fond,
And you thought it the most becoming she had ever
donned.
Yes, and what was the result?
The dress was never again seen because some other kind
of dress was immediately decreed by the couturier's cult.
And that's what happens to the clothes that she would
still be looking marvellous in if her claim that she
dresses just to please you had any validity,
But any male who comments on the fact becomes about
as popular around the house as asafoetidity,

So then she goes out and buys a garment with the lines of
   a birthday cake or a hat worn by a royalty of Britain,
And the only way you can explain anybody's buying it is
   that when they boughten it they were litten,
And you are asked how you like it, and you either say or
   don't say, depending on your daring,
But whatever you say it doesn't make any difference
   because it's going to be worn because it's what all the
   other women are wearing,
Because a woman's mental processes are harder to understand than those of a cannibal or an angel or an elf,
And they would rather dress like every other woman and
   look terrible than dress differently and look beautiful
   as their own beautiful self.

ADMIRAL BYRD

Huzza Huzza for Admiral Byrd
About whom many fine things I have heard.
Huzza Huzza for his gallant crew
About whom many fine things I have heard too.
Huzza Huzza for their spirit of Adventia
So very different from Senile Dementia.
And another Huzza for the U.S.A.
Which produces so many heroes like they.

ABSENCE MAKES THE HEART GROW HEART TROUBLE

I know a girl who is in Paris, France,
And I fear that every evening she goes out to dance,
And she ought to be pining for the undersigned,
But I fear that nothing is further from her mind,
And what is very suspicious, her letters say that she is
    being very quiet,
But my nerves deny it,
And I am unhappily sure that she is drinking champagne
    with aristocrats,
And exchanging cynicisms with sophistocrats.
She goes walking in the Bois
With elegant young men who are not moi.
She is receiving compliments from ambassadors,
And riding in fiacres with foreign agents who cry that for
    her they would betray the secrets of their lords and
    massadors.
Artists to have her pose for them are clamouring,
Tenors and symphony conductors tempt her with their
    entire repertoire from Pagliacci to Götterdämmerung;
Argentines and Brazilians
Seek to dazzle her with their dazzling millions;
Men of the world with etchings and monocles
Plead with her to become part of their personal chronicles;
Aides and equerries try to explain without too much
    bluntness and yet without too much shyness
The advantages a girl or a tailor enjoys when he or she is
    entitled to the subtitle of By Appointment to His Royal
    Highness.
Trips abroad are very nice for Davis Cup teams and
    Olympic teams, and that's about all you can say for
    them,
Because I think that when you are fond of somebody you
    would rather be with them than away from them,

So I wish that time would suddenly advance,
Because I want to be standing on the dock trying to find
    somebody on deck who will undoubtedly be wearing
    a terribly smart and perfectly terrible hat which she
    bought in Paris, France.

EVERYBODY MAKES POETS

Poets aren't very useful,
Because they aren't very consumeful or very produceful.
Even poets of great promise
Don't contribute much to trade and commerce,
To which, indeed, even poets of great achievement
Are a positive bereavement,
Because they aren't very sensible,
Because they think buying and selling are cheap and lousy
    and reprehensible,
And this is a topic about which poets are people to whom
    you cannot tell anything,
Because they are people who cannot afford to buy any-
    thing and are seldom glib enough to sell anything,
So there is some excuse for the way they feel,
Because they have seen lots of sunsets but no big deals so
    it follows naturally that they consider a sunset more
    important than a big deal.
Some poets are bitter,
But they are preferable to the poets who are all of a
    twitter,
But even the poets who are all of a twitter are as depend-
    able as Rotary
Compared to what each of them has around him which is
    a rapturous coterie,
Because every poet is threatened constantly by one dis-
    aster,
Which is that a lot of otherwise thwarted male and
    female ladies will go around calling him Master,
And then there is nothing to do but surrender,
And then it is good-bye old poetry, hello old theosophy
    and gender,
And yet on the other hand if a poet isn't fed by a lot of
    male and female ladies who are affected,
Why, until long after he is dead or gets the Pulitzer
    Prize, why he is neglected.

But the worst thing that can happen to a poet

Is to be ashamed of poetry as poetry so that he excuses himself for writing it by writing it sociologically in terms of Moscow or Detroet,

Which is something I regret,

Because it is like a preacher taking a couple of highballs and telling a dirty story just to prove that he is a hail fellow well met,

So my advice to mothers is if you are the mother of a poet don't gamble on the chance that future generations may crown him

Follow your original impulse and drown him.

MR PEACHEY'S PREDICAMENT
or
NO MOT PARADES

Once there was a man named Mr Peachey and he lived on
   Park Avenue and played the harp and was an eligible
   bachelor but his social life was hapless,
And he thought at first it was because his parents came
   from Indianapless,
But one day he awoke from a troubled nap,
And said I am tired of this hapless social life, what I want
   is a social life simply teeming with hap.
It can't be, he said, that I don't play the harp enough,
I wonder if just possibly my wits are not sharp enough.
I know that I'm pretty noted
But I've never been quoted;
Perhaps the solution for me
Is some iridescent repartee;
Suppose before I next dine out I compose a series of
   epigrams of searing astringency
And then I shall be ready for a quip for any conversational
   contingency.
So he composed a series of epigrams of indubitable
   variety,
And went to dine with some people way up in society.
And in the taxi he memorized his lines and held a solo
   rehearsal,
And he was delighted, because he said some people's
   humour is specialized but mine is universal.
There may well be a Mr Shoemaker there who has divorced
   a beautiful rich virtuous wife for a debt-ridden hideous
   wife with a past,
And I'll say Shoemaker you should have stuck to your last;
And suppose somebody remarks that the hostess looks
   like a Titian I bring them up short,
I can answer, Looks like a Titian, eh? Do you mean
   beaut- or mort-?

46

And I'll go right on and say While we are on the subject
of waltzes I'd like to play a little Haydn for you, and
I'll go to the piano and grope at the keys and then
look up impishly and speak,
And say I really don't know whether I'm playing Haydn or
Haydn seek.
Then after the laughter has died down I shall approach
some Yale man who has just returned from abroad
whom I wish to embarrass
And I'll ask him how he enjoyed the Boola-Boolavards of
Paris.
Oh, said Mr Peachey gleefully, the days of my hapless
social life are over, I cannot help but be a wow,
I wish I was at the party right now.
But when he got to the party his hostess, who didn't
look like a Titian at all, she looked like a Dali, was
quite sharp,
And sent him right back to his Park Avenue apartment
to get his harp,
And today he is living in the old family mansion in
Indianapless
Where I'm sorry to say his social life is just as hapless.

GOOD-BYE, OLD YEAR, YOU OAF
or
WHY DON'T THEY PAY THE BONUS?

Many of the three hundred and sixty-five days of the year
 are followed by dreadful nights but one night is by far,
 oh yes, by far the worst,

And that, my friends, is the night of December the thirty-first.

Man can never get it through his head that he is born to be
 not a creditor but a debtor;

Man always thinks the annual thought that just because
 last year was terrible next year is bound to be better.

Man is a victim of dope

In the incurable form of hope;

Man is a blemishless Pollyanna,

And is convinced that the advent of every New Year will
 place him in possession of a bumper crop of manna.

Therefore Man fills himself up with a lot of *joie de vivre*

And goes out to celebrate New Year's Ivre;

Therefore millions of respectable citizens who just a week
 before have been perfectly happy to sit at home and be
 cosily Christmas carolized

Consider it a point of honour to go out on the town and
 get themselves paralyzed;

There the whistles blow toot toot and the bells ring ding
 ding and the confetti goes confetti confetti at midnight
 on the thirty-first of December,

And on January first the world is full of people who
 either can't and wish they could, or can and wish
 they couldn't remember.

They never seem to learn from experience;

They keep on doing it year after year from the time they
 are puling infants till they are doddering octogenerience.

My goodness, if there's anything in heredity and environ-
 ment

How can people expect the newborn year to manifest
 any culture or refironment?

Every New Year is the direct descendant, isn't it, of a long
line of proven criminals?
And you can't turn it into a philanthropist by welcoming
it with cocktails and champagne any more successfully
than with prayer books and hyminals.
Every new year is a country as barren as the old one, and
it's no use trying to forage it;
Every new year is incorrigible; then all I can say is for
Heaven's sakes, why go out of your way to incorrage it?

FRIDAY COMES AROUND SO QUICKLY

How oft I think I do not wish
Ever again to feed on fish.
Though known as one who seldom belittles
Anything in the shape of victuals,
I find it easy not to crave
These denizens of stream and wave.
Where else does life hold such a letdown
As when you at the table setdown;
You've toiled all day with main and might,
You have a congressman's appetite;
Your palate it would barely tickle
To eat the buffalo off a nickel,
And after that the Indian chief;
But what you really want is beef.
Rich dripping slabs of roasted kine,
Thick as your thumb and red as wine;
Or maybe a steak that sizzles like sin,
All crisp outside, all juicy within;
You could cope with platters of chops and chickens
Like an eater out of Scott or Dickens;
You don't care what you get to eat
As long as it's meat and still more meat.
The meal is ready, the hands are dealt—
And you catch the eye of a sneering smelt.
Oh, speak to me not of trout or bluefish,
I remain unmoved and coldly aloofish;
Salmon and mackerel tempt me not,
Nor the pompano nor the Norfolk spot;
The pallid cod and the finnan haddie
Merely irk this carnivorous laddie.
Whether captured by net or by baited hook,
Fish never lose that fishlike look;

Season away, they never waver,
Never surrender their fishlike flavour.
Fish are relished by other fish,
Seagulls think them a savoury dish,
But I will take them, if taken at all,
Mounted and hung on a bar-room wall.

LITTLE MISS MUFFET SAT ON A PROPHET — AND QUITE RIGHT, TOO!

I am sure that if anybody into the condition of humanity cares to probe,
Why they will agree with the prophet Job,
Because the prophet Job said that man that is born of woman is of few days and full of trouble, that's what was said by the prophet Job,
And the truth of that statement can be confirmed by anybody who cares to probe.
So you would think that being born to trouble and woe, man would be satisfied,
And indeed that just by being born at all his passion for trouble would be gratisfied.
But is man content to leave bad enough alone?
Not so, he has to go out and create a lot more trouble and woe of his own.
Man knows very well that rheumatism and measles and ice and fog and pain and senility and sudden death are his for the asking, and, indeed, his whether he asks for them or not,
But when it comes to agony, man is a glutton and a sot,
His appetite for punishment is immense,
And any torture that Nature overlooked, he invents.
There is no law of Nature that compels a man to drink too much,
Or even to think too much,
And when Nature looked at her handiwork, for purposes of her own she certainly added gender to it,
But she didn't order everybody to dive overboard and surrender to it,
Yes, it may have been Nature who induced two people to love each other and end up by marrying each other,
But it is their own idea when they begin to lovingly torment and harry each other.

And it may have been Nature who developed the mosquito
and the gnat and the midge,
But man developed golf and bridge,
And Nature may have thought up centipedes and ants,
But man all by himself thought up finance,
So this prophet will utter just one utterance instead of
uttering them like the prophet Job in baker's twelves,
Which utterance is that people could survive their natural
trouble all right if it weren't for the trouble they make
for themselves.

REMINISCENT REFLECTION

When I consider how my life is spent
I hardly ever repent.

SONG FOR PIER SOMETHING OR OTHER

Steamer, steamer, outward bound,
Couldn't you, wouldn't you turn around?
Mightn't you double on your track?
Mightn't you possibly bring her back?
No, says the steamer, No, no, no!
We go, says the steamer, go, go, go!
Who, says the steamer, Who are you?
Boo! says the steamer.
Boo!

Steamer, steamer, are you sure
You can carry her secure?
Emerge from ice and storm and fog
With an uneventful log?
Chance, says the steamer, I am chance!
Chance, says the steamer, That's romance!
Who, says the steamer, Who are you?
Boo! says the steamer.
Boo!

Steamer, steamer, hard and splendid,
Goddess unwittingly offended,
Are the males who prowl your decks
Attractive to the other sex?
Wait, says the steamer, Sit and wait.
Fate, says the steamer, I am Fate.
Who, says the steamer, Who are you?
Boo! says the steamer.
Boo!

Steamer, cogitate a while,
Before you smile your final smile.
Seven days are yours to mock;
Steamer, wait until you dock.

Wait till she is safe ashore,
Steamer I do not adore!
Boo, says the steamer, and double boo!
Who, says the steamer,
Are you?

Steamer, steamer, I am he
Whose *raison d'être* you bore to sea,
And I wish you junkets and week-end cruises
With passengers hiccuping where the booze is
And Hyde Park Roosevelts, beamish and gay,
And Roosevelts from Oyster Bay.
Steamer, lightly you weighed your anchor.
Try so lightly to weigh my rancor.
You who carried her off so boldly
Shall pay for it hotly, pay for it coldly,
With blistering hurricanes, frosty gales,
With tangoing octopods, crooning whales—
Steamer, as soon as she is off you,
Then I shall really cut loose and scoff you!
When she has said farewell to the purser,
I'll curse you meaner, I'll curse you worser,
Pooh! says the steamer, Pooh for you!
Toodle-de-oodle-de-oo!

I can't say that I feel particularly one way or the other
    towards bell-boys,
But I do admit that I haven't much use for the it's-just-as-
    well boys,
The cheery souls who drop around after every catastrophe
    and think they are taking the curse off
By telling you about somebody who is even worse off.
No matter how deep and dark your pit, how dank your
    shroud,
Their heads are heroically unbloody and unbowed.
If you have just lost the one love of your life, there is no
    possible doubt of it,
They tell you there are as good fish in the sea as ever
    came out of it.
If you are fined ten dollars for running past a light when
    you didn't but the cop says you did,
They say Cheer up think of the thousand times you ran
    past them and didn't get caught so you're really ten
    thousand bucks ahead, Hey old kid?
If you lose your job they tell you how lucky you are
    that you've saved up a little wealth
And then when the bank folds with the savings they tell
    you you sure are lucky to still have your health.
Life to them is just one long happy game,
At the conclusion of which the One Great Scorer writes
    not whether you won it or lost it, but how you played
    it, against your name.
Kismet, they say, it's Fate.   What is to be, will be.   Buck
    up!   Take heart!
Kismet indeed!   Nobody can make me grateful for Paris
    green in the soup just by reassuring me that it comes
    that way Allah carte.

LOVE FOR SALE

Waiter, remove yon wistful verse;
It might be better, it might be worse,
But I think that what I'm tiredest of
Is poets who write of love.
Love victorious,
Love maltreated,
Love uproarious,
Love defeated,
Love just starting,
Love ethereal,
Love departing,
Love material,
Love eternal,
And, most explicit,
Love infernal,
And love illicit,
Love that's slighted
And love Platonic,
Love requited,
Love embryonic,
Love athletic
And love repressed,
Love cosmetic
And love confessed.
I think that what I am tiredest of
Is people who write of love.

I think that what I am tiredest of
Is dramas that drip with love.
Love unspoken,
Love unselfish,
Love just woken,
Love coy and elfish,
Love tormented,
Love celestial,

Love resented,
Love low and bestial,
Love embarrassed,
Love ambitious,
Love sad and harrassed,
Love surreptitious,
Love in Chile,
Love in China,
Or in Scilly
And South Carolina,
Love in Manhattan,
Love that rages
In French and Latin
Across the ages.
Waiter, remove yon dripping dramas,
And bring me Pickwick and my old pyjamas.

ARE YOU A SNODGRASS?

It is possible that most individual and international social and economic collisions

Result from humanity's being divided into two main divisions,

Both of which are irreconcilable,

And neither is by the other beguilable;

Their lives are spent in mutual interference,

And yet you cannot tell them apart by their outward appearance.

Indeed the only way in which to tell one group from the other you are able

Is to observe them at table,

Because the only visible way in which one group from the other varies

Is in its treatment of the cream and sugar on cereal and berries.

Group A, which we will call the Swozzlers because it is a very suitable name, I deem,

First applies the sugar and then swozzles it all over the place pouring on the cream,

And as fast as they put the sugar on they swozzle it away,

For such thriftlessness means nothing to ruthless egotists like they,

They just continue to scoop and swozzle and swozzle and scoop,

Until there is nothing left for the Snodgrasses, or second group.

A Snodgrass is a kind, handsome, intelligent person who pours the cream on first,

And then deftly sprinkles the sugar over the cereal or berries after they have been properly immersed,

Thus assuring himself that the sugar will remain on the cereal and berries where it can do some good, which is his wish,

Instead of being swozzled away to the bottom of the dish.

The facts of the case for the Snodgrasses are so self-evident that it is ridiculous to debate them,

But this is unfortunate for the Snodgrasses as it only causes the sinister and vengeful Swozzlers all the more to hate them.

Swozzlers are irked by the superior Snodgrass intelligence and nobility

And they lose no opportunity of inflicting on them every kind of incivility.

If you read that somebody has been run over by an automobile

You may be sure that the victim was a Snodgrass, and a Swozzler was at the wheel.

Swozzlers start wars and Snodgrasses get killed in them,

Swozzlers sell water-front lots and Snodgrasses get malaria when they try to build in them.

Swozzlers invent fashionable diets and drive Snodgrasses crazy with tables of vitamins and calories,

Swozzlers go to Congress and think up new taxes and Snodgrasses pay their salaries,

Swozzlers bring tigers back alive and Snodgrasses get eaten by anacondas,

Snodgrasses are depositors and Swozzlers are absconders,

Swozzlers hold straight flushes when Snodgrasses hold four of a kind,

Swozzlers step heavily on the toes of Snodgrasses' shoes as soon as they are shined.

Whatever achievements Snodgrasses achieve, Swozzlers always top them;

Snodgrasses say Stop me if you've heard this one, and Swozzlers stop them.

Swozzlers are teeming with useful tricks of the trade that are not included in standard university curricula;

The world in general is their oyster, and Snodgrasses in particular.

So I hope for your sake, dear reader, that you are a
    Swozzler, but I hope for everybody else's sake that you
    are not,
And I also wish that everybody else was a nice amiable
    Snodgrass too, because then life would be just one long
    sweet harmonious mazurka or gavotte.

ARTHUR BRISBANE

Mr Arthur Brisbane
Considers his country's bane his bane,
He vigorously combats disloyalty,
And deprecates royalty,
And though his speech is somewhat informal,
He is a staunch advocate of the normal.
He can pen an editorial
As noble and succinct as the Lincoln Memorial
And in his column, which is widely syndicated,
The man in the street is vindicated.
Because he thought of putting LITTLE words in BIG letters,
He is now one of our betters.
He can sit for hour after hour
In a tastily gotten-up flat in the Ritz Tower,
Of which he is owner and proprietor
Because he is such a good wrietor.
I wonder if you and I could assume similar attitudes
If we too knew how to pound the multitude with plati-
    tudes.

DEAR GODMOTHER; I HOPE SHE
·BRUISES EASY!

Good morrow, my little man, do you know who I am?
  I am your fairy godmother, that's who,
And can I fix you up with anything you want? Well, can
  a duck swim, and can a cow moo?
Yes, little man, just one wave of my good old wand,
And you shall have anything of which you are fond.
Is it glass slippers you desire, or a cloak of darkness, or
  three wishes, or seven-league boots?
The minute my little man says the word, why the works
  are what godmother shoots.
Perhaps you would prefer
To be a delightful engaging witty *raconteur*,
So I shall give you the power of remembering all the
  comical anecdotes you hear,
Instead of having them go in one and out the other ear.
Is your employment beginning to pall?
Very well, you shall have the choice either of enjoying
  your work or else not having to work at all.
Do you long to excel in repartee, do you yearn for a
  little more dignity and a little less paunch?
Godson, I hereby give you *carte blanche*.
You shall always hold the major suits and your opponents
  the minors,
And you shall be able to drink the coffee that confronts
  you on diners;
In the race to beat the traffic light you shall trounce
  whoever you race with,
And when you stay at hotels you shall find that the
  bathrooms are actually supplied with washcloths to
  wash your face with;
Your ship shall be constantly coming into harbour,
And you shall know how to talk to a barber;
Your taxes shall be infinitesimal,

And the Department of Internal Revenue shall say you
    need never pay a tax again because your return is a
    masterpiece right down to the last decimal;
When head waiters attempt to seat you under the electric
    fan by the service door you shall know how to quash
    them with a snub that rankles,
And when you skate you shall skate on your skates in-
    stead of on your ankles;
Your children shall not be acrobats and their I.Q.s shall
    be plus and their behaviour problems minus;
And you shall be able to step into a ready-made suit and
    it shall look as if it had been specially tailored for you
    by a tailor who tailors By Appointment to His Royal
    Highnus;
And hark ye, godson, I save the best for the last, for lo
    and behold!
You shall never catch cold.
Oh, and PS., godson, just two more words before god-
    mother disappears, but godmother has an idea they
    may knock you for a gool:
April Fool!

FRAGMENTS FROM THE JAPANESE

I

There was an old man of Calcutta,
Who coated his tonsils with butta,
Thus converting his snore
From a thunderous roar
To a soft, oleaginous mutta.

II

There was an old gossip named Baird,
Who said, 'What I could say, if I dared!
I will say it, in fact,
Though I die in the act'—
So she said it, and nobody cared.

III

A nasty old man on a boat
Inquired, 'Are you sure it will float?'
After which he cried 'Boo!'
At the terrified crew,
And retired to his cabin to gloat.

IV

There was a brave girl of Connecticut
Who signalled the train with her pecticut,
Which the papers defined
As presence of mind,
But deplorable absence of ecticut.

V

There was an old man in a trunk,
Who inquired of his wife, 'Am I drunk?'
She replied with regret,
'I'm afraid so, my pet,'
And he answered, 'It's just as I thunk.'

VI

There was an old man of Schoharie,
Who settled himself in a quarry.
And those who asked why
Got the simple reply,
'Today is the day of the soirée.'

VII

There was a young lady named Harris,
Whom nothing could ever embarrass,
Till the bath salts one day
In the tub where she lay
Turned out to be plaster of Paris.

VIII

There was an old maid of Madrid
Who sat on the mayor and slid,
While chanting aloud
To the curious crowd,
'I told him I would, and I did!'

IX

There was an old miser named Clarence,
Who simonized both of his parents.
'The initial expense,'
He remarked, 'is immense,
But I'll save it on wearance and tearance.'

X

There was a young man of Newhaven,
Who was called a poltroon and a craven,
Till he startled his friends
Into making amends
By loudly reciting 'The Raven.'

XI

A bugler named Dougal MacDougal
Found ingenious ways to be frugal.
He learned how to sneeze
In various keys,
Thus saving the price of a bugle.

EPILOGUE TO MOTHER'S DAY, WHICH IS TO BE PUBLISHED ON ANY DAY BUT MOTHER'S DAY

Mothers! Mothers! It was visions of mothers that had
    been relentlessly haunting me,
Wherever I turned I saw misty mothers sitting around
    taunting me.
It was battalions of irritated spectres that blanched my
    face and gave me this dull and lustre-lack eye,
Night and day I was surrounded by mothers, from Mrs
    Whistler, Senior, to Mrs Dionne and from Yale the
    mother of men to Niobe and the mother of the Gracchi.
I resented this supernatural visitation, these are not the
    dark ages, these are the days of modernity,
I wilted before this intrusion of miasmic maternity.
Mothers, I cried, oh myriads of mothers, I can stand it
    no longer, what can I do for you?
Do you want me to have you exorcized, do you want me
    to pray for you, do you want me to say Boo for you?
I know you are major figures in history's Who's Whom.
But I wish you would go away because your company is
    flattering but I would rather have your room.
Then they replied in hollow chorus,
We have thought of something that we want to have
    published but we can't write so you will have to write
    it for us,
And if you write it we will leave you alone,
And if you don't write it we will haunt you brain from
    skull and flesh from bone,
So I acquiesced and the ghastly horde dictated to me and
    I wrote it,
And a promise is a promise and an army of ghostly
    mothers is an army of ghostly mothers, so I quote it:—
M is for the preliminary million-dollar advertising ap-
    propriation,

O means that she is always white-haired, bespectacled and at least eighty-five years old,

T is for Telegraph message number 31B which contains a tastefully blended expression of sentiment and congratulation,

H is for the coast-to-coast questionnaire which proved conclusively that seven-and-one-half citizens out of every ten with incomes of $5,000 a year or better would rather have their mother than gold.

E is for the Elephants which everybody is very glad didn't sit down on their mothers,

R is for Rosemary which is for Remembrance of the fact that a mother is one thing that you will never have more than one of,

Put them all together and before you can say H. St C. Wellington Carruthers, they spell the second of two things that everybody who loves their mother only once a year and then only at the instigation of the Chamber of Commerce is a son of.

I'LL BE UP IN A MINUTE

Oh some men want their vanished youth
And some a million dollars,
And expensive cars and big cigars,
And shirts with silken collars.
Some wish to paint the beautifulest,
Some wish to paint the oddest;
But never have I aspired so high;
My dream is meek and modest.

It's ten more minutes in bed
With a yaw and a yawn and a yaw,
Yes, ten more minutes in bed,
When the sunlight's bricht and braw;
To swoon like a weeping willow
With a ho and a hum and a ho,
Once more across my pillow,
And to roll from to to fro;
To thwart the meddlesome rising bell
With a blanket o'er my head;
To yawn at the dawn and carry on
For ten more minutes in bed.

Oh sleep at eve is a blessed thing,
And sleep at night is blesseder,
And poets leap to write of sleep,
Death's brother and ambassador.
I welcome sleep at any hour,
I have, since I was born;
But the sleep I love all sleep above
Is a little more sleep at morn.

Oh, ten more minutes in bed,
With a yaw and a yawn and a yaw,
Just ten more minutes in bed,
For aged muscles to thaw.

To stretch like a drowsy feline,
With a ho and a hum and a ho,
To follow a flowery beeline
To the land where the good dreams go.
Let robots listen to the rising bell
And spring to earn their bread;
I'll yawn at the dawn and carry on
For ten more minutes in bed.

People by whom I am riled
Are people who go around wishing O that Time would backward turn backward and again make them a child.
Either they have no sense, or else they go around repeating something they have heard, like a parakeet,
Or else they deliberately prevarikete,
Because into being a marathon dancer or a chiropodist or a tea-taster or a certified public accountant I could not be beguiled,
But I could sooner than I could into being again a child,
Because being a child is not much of a pastime,
And I don't want any next time because I remember the last time.
I do not wish to play with my toes,
Nor do I wish to have codliver oil spooned down my throat or albolene pushed up my nose.
I don't want to be plopped at sundown into a crib or a cradle
And if I don't go to sleep right away be greeted with either a lullaby or an upbraidal.
I can think of nothing worse
Than never being out of sight of a parent or nurse:
Yes, that is the part that I don't see how they survive it,
To have their private life so far from private.
Furthermore, I don't want to cry for the moon,
And I do want to hold my own spoon;
I have more ambitious ideas of a lark
Than to collect pebbles in my hat or be taken for a walk in the park;
I should hate to be held together with safety pins instead of buttons and suspenders and belts,
And I should particularly hate being told every time I was doing something I liked that it was time to do something else.

So it's pooh for the people who want Time to make
them a child again because I think they must already
be a child again or else they would stand up and
own up
That it's much more fun to be a grown-up.

A WARNING TO WIVES

'The outcome of the trial is another warning that if
you must kill someone, you should spare the person
possessing life insurance. . . . Figures are available to
show that convictions are much more common in
"insurance murders" than in other types of homicides.'
—Daily newspaper.

Speak gently to your husband, mum,
And encourage all his sneezes;
That nasty cough may carry him off,
If exposed to draughts and breezes.
And suppose the scoundrel lingers on,
And insists on being cured;
Well, it isn't a sin if a girl steps in—
Unless the brute's insured.

Oh, the selfishness of men, welladay, welladay!
Oh the cowards, oh the misers, oh the mice!
Egotistically they strive to keep themselves alive,
And insurance is their scurviest device.
Insurance!
It's insurance
That tries a person's temper past endurance.
Yet it's safer, on the whole,
To practise self-control
If there's apt to be a question of insurance.

Arsenic soup is a dainty soup,
But not if he's paid his premium,
Or a ·32 in a pinch will do,
If you're bored with the epithalamium.
But to make acquittal doubly sure—
No maybes, no perhapses—
You'll do well to wait to expunge your mate
Until his policy lapses.

The hypocrisy of men, welladay, welladay!
Whited sepulchres are much to be preferred.
They claim it's for their wives they evaluate their lives,
But it's fatal if you take them at their word.
Insurance!
Oh, insurance!
What holds potential widows fast in durance?
Not the Adlers and the Freuds,
But the Mutuals and Lloyds,
And the jury's evil mind about insurance.

NO WONDER OUR FATHERS DIED

Does anybody mind if I don't live in a house that is quaint?

Because, for one thing, quaint houses are generally houses where plumbing ain't,

And while I don't hold with fanatical steel-and-glass modernistic bigots,

Still, I do think that it simplifies life if you live it surrounded by efficient pipes and faucets and spigots.

I admit that wells and pumps and old oaken buckets are very nice in a poem or ode,

But I feel that in literature is where they should have their permanent abode,

Because suppose you want a bath,

It is pleasanter to be able to take it without leaving a comfortable stuffy room and going out into the bracing fresh air and bringing back some water from the end of a path.

Another thing about which I am very earnest,

Is that I do like a house to be properly furnaced,

Because if I am out in the bracing fresh air I expect to be frozen,

But to be frigid in a stuffy room isn't what I would have chosen.

And when you go to bed in a quaint house the whole house grumbles and mutters,

And you are sure the walls will be shattered by clattering shutters.

At least you hope it's the shutters but you fear it's a gang of quaint ghosts warming up for twelve o'clock,

And you would lock yourself snugly in but the quaint old key won't turn in the quaint old lock,

So you would pull the bedclothes snugly up over your head and lie there till a year from next autumn,

Were it not a peculiarity of bedclothes in quaint houses that if you pull them up on top, why your feet stick out at the bautum,

But anyhow you find a valley among the hilltops of your
mattress and after a while slumber comes softly stealing,
And that is when you feel a kiss on your cheek and you
think maybe it is a goodnight kiss from your guardian
angel, but it isn't, it's a leak in the ceiling.
Oh, I yield to none in my admiration of the hardy colon-
ists and their hardy spouses,
But I still feel that their decadent descendants build more
comfortable houses.

PARSLEY FOR VICE-PRESIDENT!

I'd like to be able to say a good word for parsley, but I can't,

And after all what can you find to say for something that even the dictionary dismisses as a biennial umbelliferous plant?

Speaking of which, I don't know how the dictionary figures it as biennial, it is biennial my eye, it is like the poor and the iniquitous,

Because it is always with us, because it is permanent and ubiquitous.

I will not venture to deny that it is umbelliferous,

I will only add that it is of a nasty green colour, and faintly odoriferous,

And I hold by my complaint, though every cook and hostess in the land indict me for treason for it,

That parsley is something that as a rhymer I can find no rhyme for it and as an eater I can find no reason for it.

Well, there is one sin for which a lot of cooks and hostesses are some day going to have to atone,

Which is that they can't bear to cook anything and leave it alone.

No, they see food as something to base a lot of beautiful dreams and romance on,

Which explains lamb chops with pink and blue pants on.

Everything has to be decorated and garnished

So the guests will be amazed and astarnished,

And whatever you get to eat, it's sprinkled with a lot of good old umbelliferous parsley looking as limp and wistful as Lillian Gish,

And it is limpest, and wistfulest, and also thickest, on fish.

Indeed, I think maybe one reason for the disappearance of Enoch Arden

Was that his wife had an idea that mackerel tasted better if instead of looking like mackerel it looked like a garden.

Well, anyhow, there's the parsley cluttering up your food,
And the problem is to get it off without being rude,
And first of all you try to scrape it off with your fork,
And you might as well try to shave with a cork,
And then you surreptitiously try your fingers,
And you get covered with butter and gravy, but the parsley
lingers,
And you turn red and smile at your hostess and compli-
ment her on the recipe and ask her where she found it,
And then you return to the parsley and as a last resort you
try and eat around it,
And the hostess says, Oh, you are just picking at it, is
there something wrong with it?
So all you can do is to eat it all up, and the parsley along
with it,
And now is the time for all good parsleyphobes to come
to the aid of the menu and exhibit their gumption,
And proclaim that any dish that has either a taste or an
appearance that can be improved by parsley in *ipso
facto* a dish unfit for human consumption.

HAPPY DAYS, ELMER!

Elmer stops me in the street,
He fastens to my arm;
Elmer's words are words of heat,
I view him with alarm.
Elmer's eyes are eyes that glisten;
When he talks, he pants;
To Elmer's speech I do not listen;
Know it in advance.

Somewhere, somehow, something terrible,
Something altogether unbearable,
Squashes a dictator, squashes a homebody,
Something dreadful happens to somebody, AND—
Bombs are exploding like banks,
Banks are exploding like bombs,
The Russians are mad at the Yanks,
Kippurs are torn from their Yoms.
The world is adrift in a fog;
Myself, I am frankly appalled;
But Elmer is gaily agog;
Yes, Elmer is simply enthralled.
Says Elmer, the times are portentous,
We are favoured to be on the spot
At a moment, he says, so momentous—
I trust he's momentously shot.

I stop Elmer in the street,
Arm in arm we walk;
Elmer must have grown effete;
He listens while I talk.
Elmer's eyes are eyes that pop;
When I talk, he pants;
I orate without a stop;
Prepared it in advance.

Somewhere, somehow, something tedious,
Something stupidly yes-indeedious,
Something tiresome will happen to somebody,
Bore a dictator, weary a homebody, AND—
The Slavs will yawn at the Letts,
Ennui will grow out of chaos,
We'll sleepily mention our debts,
Our debtors will sleepily pay us.
Nothing will rise or fall
In a humdrum world and drowsy.
Elmer won't like it at all,
But life will be much less lousy.
I'm ragged from critical crises,
And I beg with my vanishing breath,
At the moment, O Lord, I want to be bored—
I want to be bored to death!

THE PARTY NEXT DOOR

I trust I am not a spoil-sport, but there is one thing I
deplore,
And that is a party next door,
If there is anything that gives me tantrums galore
It is a party next door.
I do not know how we came into this world, or what
for,
But it was not, I am sure, to listen to a party next door.
I am by nature very fond of everybody, even my neigh-
bours,
And I think it only right that they should enjoy some
kind of diversion after their labours,
But why don't they get their diversion by going to the
movies or the Little Theatre or the Comédie française
or the Commedia dell' arte?
Why do they always have to be giving a party?
You may think you have heard a noise because you have
heard an artillery barrage or an avalanche or the sub-
way's horrendous roar,
But you have never really heard anything until you have
heard a party next door,
You may have survived the impact of a gangster's bullet
or a hit-and-run driver or a bolt of lightning or the
hammer of Thor,
But you really don't know what an impact is until you
have felt the impact of a party next door.
A party next door never really gets going until you are
trying for some much-needed sleep,
And when it does get going, why awake is much easier
than your temper to keep.
At a party next door the guests stampede like elephants
in wooden shoes and gallop like desperate polo players,
And all the women are coloratura sopranos and all the
men are train announcers and hogcallers and saxo-
phone solo players.

They all have screamingly funny stories to tell to each other,

And half of them get at one end of the house and half of them get at the other end of the yard and then they yell to each other.

The spirit is one of lawlessness and mockery,

And its audible symbols are giggles and squeals and guffaws and splintering furniture and crashing crockery.

And even if the patrolman looks in from his beat they do not moderate or stop,

No, they just seduce the cop.

And at last you manage to doze off by the dawn's early light,

And they wake you up all over again shouting good night,

And the host roars out to people to come back in for a final cup,

And the windows rattle with horns blowing for wives who can't find their bags, and engines being warmed up,

And whether it consists of two quiet old ladies dropping in for a game of bridge or a lot of revellers getting really sort of out-of-bounds-like,

That's what a party next door always sounds like,

So when you see somebody with a hoarse voice and a pallid face and eyes bleary and red-rimmed and sore,

It doesn't mean they've been on a party themselves, no, it probably means that they have experienced a party next door.

HEARTS AND FLOWERS
or
WHAT I KNOW ABOUT BOLIVAR BLACK

I do not care for Bolivar Black,
And I think that I never shall;
A shiver goes rippling up my back
When Bolivar calls me Pal.
I am commonly captain of my soul,
But my head is bowed and bloody,
No joy can I find in human kind,
When Bolivar calls me Buddy.

His smile is broad as a non-stop flight
From Timbuctoo to Texas,
And a heart as warm as a desert storm
Sizzles his solar plexus.
Bolivar's love for his fellow man
Is deep as the rolling ocean,
And the favourite scent of the Orient
Enlivens his shaving lotion.

He's wild about children, people say,
And devoted to widows and orphans;
When he speaks as he should of motherhood
His sonorous accent sorftens.
He scatters crumbs for our feathered friends,
He is kind to kittens and puppies,
And his salary cheque is at the beck
Of a prodigal tribe of guppies.

The beggars gamble among themselves
For the right to beg of Bolivar;
And the burglars go with a tale of woe
Instead of a big revolivar.

He lavishes fruit on his travelling friends,
And flowers upon the ill;
When a dozen dine and order wine,
Bolivar snatches the bill.

His virtues bloom like the buds in May,
His faults, I believe, are few,
But whether you find him gold or clay
Depends on the point of view.
So you may care for Bolivar Black,
And his generous actions quote;
My praise is checked when I recollect
My name on Bolivar's note.

THE BANQUET

Oh, here we are at the mammoth banquet
To honour the birth of the great Bosanquet!
Oh give a look at the snowy napery,
The costly flowers, the sumptuous drapery,
Row on row of silver utensils
Poised for action like salesmen's pencils,
Waiters gaudy as sugar plums,
Every waiter with seven thumbs,
Stream upon stream of gaudy bunting,
And lady commuters lion hunting,
The gleaming teeth at the speaker's table,
The clattering, chattering, battering babel.
Sit we here in the great unquiet
And brood awhile on the evening's diet.
As soggy and dull as good advice,
The butter floats in the melting ice.
In a neighbouring morgue, beyond salvation,
The celery waits identification.
Huddled thick in an open vault,
Mummified peanuts moult their salt.
Out of the napkin peers a roll,
With the look of a lost and hardened soul.
The cocktail sauce, too weak to roister,
Fails to enliven the tepid oyster.
The consommé, wan as Elizabeth Barrett,
Washes over a drowning carrot.
Next, with its sauce of Mdvi-Tarter,
The sole, or flounder, or is it a garter?
Ho! fresh from the ranchos of Avignon,
O'Sullivan's Rubber filet mignon;
Parsley potatoes, as tempting as soap,
String beans, hemp beans, and beans of rope.
And the waiter would sooner serve you his daughter
Than give you another glass of water.

Pineapple salad next, by George!
That ought to raise your sunken gorge!
And green ice cream, sweet frozen suet,
With nuts and raisins sprinkled through it.
At sight of vari-coloured *gâteaux*
The innards reel, as on a *bateau*.
At last the little cups belated
Of coffee dated, or inundated.
Chairs creak as half a thousand rumps
Twist them around with backward bumps,
A thousand eyes seek out, as one,
The beaming chairman on his throne.
He rises luminous through the smoke
Of banquet tobacco, or poison oak.
He bows, he coughs, he smiles a bit,
He sparkles with imitable wit—
Rabbi Ben Ezra, fly with me;
The almost worse is yet to be.
Let us arise and leave this banquet—
And by the way, Rabbi, who was Bosanquet?

SUMMERGREEN FOR PRESIDENT

Winter comes but once a year,
And when it comes it brings the doctor good cheer;
Yes, it comes but once a year but it lasts for most of it,
And you may think there is a chance it may be a mild one,
but there isn't a ghost of it.
Winter is indeed a season that I would like to apply an
uncomplimentary name to,
But I really don't mind it as much as the people who
enjoy it, or at least claim to.
Yes, some people will say ice is nicer than slush,
And to those people I say Hush.
Some people will say snow is nicer than rain,
Which is like being still unreconciled to the defeat of
James G. Blaine.
Some people still say a freeze is nicer than a thaw,
And I hope they find cold storage Japanese beetles in their
slaw.

Slush is much nicer than ice because when you step in it
you simply go splash, instead of immediately de-
positing either your posterior or your pate on it,
And also you don't have to skate on it.
Rain is much nicer than snow because you don't have to
have rain ploughs piling rain up in six-foot piles exactly
where you want to go,
And you don't have to build rain-men for the kiddies and
frolic in sleighs and sleds, and also rain is nicer because
it melts the snow.
A thaw is obviously much nicer than a freeze
Because it annoys people with skis.
And in all my life I have only known one man who
honestly liked winter better than summer,
Because every summer he used to have either his tonsils
or his appendix or something out, and every winter he
was a plumber.

ADVICE OUTSIDE A CHURCH

Dear George, behold the portentous day
When bachelorhood is put away.
Bring camphor balls and cedarwood,
For George's discarded bachelorhood;
You, as the happiest of men,
Wish not to wear it ever again.
Well, if you wish to get your wish,
Mark well my words, nor reply Tush-pish.
Today we fly, tomorrow we fall,
And lawyers make bachelors of us all.
If you desire a noisy nursery
And a golden wedding anniversary,
Scan first the bog where thousands falter:
They think the wooing ends at the altar,
And boast that one triumphant procession
Has given them permanent possession.
They simply desist from further endeavour,
And assume that their brides are theirs forever.
They do not beat them, they do no wrong to them,
But they take it for granted their brides belong to
  them.
Oh, every trade develops its tricks,
Marriage as well as politics,
Suspense is silk and complacence is shoddy,
And no one belongs to anybody.
It is pleasant, George, and necessary
To pretend the arrangement is temporary.
Thank her kindly for favours shown;
She is the lender, and she the loan;
Nor appear to notice the gradual shift
By which the loan becomes a gift.
Strong are the couples who resort
More to courtship and less to court.
And I warn you, George, for your future good,
That ladies don't want to be understood.

Women are sphinxes, Woman has writ it;
If you understand her, never admit it.
Tell her that Helen was probably beautifuller,
Call, if you will, Penelope dutifuller,
Sheba charminger, Guinevere grander
But never admit that you understand her.
Hark to the strains of Lohengrin!
Heads up, George! Go in and win!

I think those people are utterly unreliable

Who say they'd be happy on a desert island with a copy of the Biable

And Hamlet (by Shakespeare) and Don Quixote (by Cervantes)

And poems by Homer and Virgil and perhaps a thing or two of Dante's.

And furthermore, I have a feeling that if they were marooned till the millennium's dawn

Very few of us would notice that they were gone.

Perhaps they don't like my opinions any better than I like theirs,

But who cares?

If I were going to be marooned and could take only one thing along

I'd be perfectly happy if I could take the thing which is the subject of this song.

I don't mean anything that was brought either by the postman or the stork.

I mean the City of New York.

For New York is a wonder city, a veritable fairyland

With many sights not to be seen in Massachusetts or Maryland.

It is situated on the island of Manhattan

Which I prefer to such islands as Welfare or Staten.

And it is far superior

To the cities of the interior.

What if it has a heterogeneous populace?

That is one of the privileges of being a metropulace

And heterogeneous people don't go around bothering each other

And you can be reasonably sure that everything you do won't get right back to your dear old mother.

In New York beautiful girls can become more beautiful by going to Elizabeth Arden

And getting stuff put on their faces and waiting for it to
   harden
And poor girls with nothing to their names but a letter
   or two can get rich and joyous
From a brief trip to their loyous.
And anybody with a relative of whose will he is the
   beneficiary
Can do pretty well in the judiciary.
So I can say with impunity
That New York is a city of opportunity.
It also has many fine theatres and hotels,
And a lot of taxis, buses, subways, and els,
Best of all, if you don't show up at the office or at a tea
   nobody will bother their head
They will just think you are dead.
That's why I really think New York is exquisite.
It isn't all right just for a visit
But by God's Grace
I'd live in it and like it even better if you gave me the place.

I'LL HUSH IF YOU'LL HUSH

Sweet voices have been presented by Nature
To creatures of varying nomenclature.
The bird, when he unlocks his beak,
Emits a melody unique;
The lion's roar, the moo-cow's bellow,
Are clearly pitched and roundly mellow;
The squirrel's chatter, the donkey's bray,
Are fairly pleasant in their way;
While even beasts whose noises are awful
Appeal therewith to their spouses lawful.
The tomcat's miaow is curdled milk
To us, but eggnog to his ilk;
How odd that I cannot rejoice,
Though human, in the human voice.
Of sounds I think the furthest South
Is that which springs from the human mouth.
No study such despair affords
As that of human vocal cords.
Do you shudder at the type of larynx
Whence herrings issue forth as harrinks?
Do you sometimes wonder which is worse,
Verce for voice, or voise for verse?
Then how about the Oxford throat,
With its swallowed vowels and tweetering note?
There's little pleasure in the stage
Since the tired accent became the rage.
Still, if you think the stage is low,
Then, what about the radio?
The smooth and oily tongues that drip
With spurious good-fellowship,
That flood your chamber with a spasm
Of cultured cold enthusiasm?
Had I of sundry sounds my choice
I should not choose the human voice;

God knows it's bad enough alone,
Without the aid of the microphone.
It's a useful means of communication
But a paltry acoustical decoration.

I am tired of gadgets with cocktails,
I am awfully tired of gadgets with cocktails,
My heart leaps down when I behold gadgets with cock-
tails
With me they have outlived their popularity.
Gadgets with cocktails are stultified
Gadgets with cocktails are stertorous
Gadgets with cocktails are stark and stagnant
And for them I have no patience or charity.

I don't want any toast covered with vulcanized caviar
Or any soggy popcorn covered with cheesy butter or
buttery cheese,
I don't want any potato chips or Tiny Tootsie pretzels
or pretzel sticks,
And I don't want any crackers coated with meat paste or
bargain *pâté de foie gras* particularly please.

Do not hand me that plate filled with olives unripe and
overripe,
Anchovies whether curled or uncurled I have concluded
not to abide,
Kindly mail all those salted peanuts and almonds to the
Collector of Internal Revenue,
As well as all the little heart-shaped sandwiches filled
with squashy stuff that when you pick them up they
squirt out at the side.

Maybe somewhere there is somebody who would like
the stuffed eggs and diminutive frankfurters,
Or who could look the stuffed celery in the eye and
voluntarily chew it,
Maybe there is a Chinaman in China who would care
for that slab of fumigated salmon,
And that thing whatever it is all rolled up with a tooth-
pick sticking through it.

Hostesses never tire of gadgets with cocktails,
Hostesses sit around thinking up new gadgets with cock-
tails,
They prowl through the papers hunting tricky gadgets for
cocktails,
And if they don't serve more than other hostesses they are
swamped with humiliation and grief;
Gadgets with cocktails to you, my dear Mrs Marshmallow,
Gadgets with cocktails to you, Mrs Rodney St Rodney,
Gadgets with cocktails to you and all other hostesses,
And I'll take some bread and butter and a slice of rare
roast beef.

CAPTAIN JOHN SMITH

Captain John Smith
Didn't belong to the B'nai B'rith,
He was a full-blooded Briton,
The same as Boadicea and Bulwer-Lytton,
But his problem and theirs were not quite the same,
Because they didn't have to go around assuring everybody that that was their real name,
And finally he said, This business of everybody raising their eyebrows when I register at an inn is getting very boring,
So I guess I'll go exploring,
So he went and explored the River James,
Where they weren't as particular then as they are now about names,
And he went for a walk in the forest,
And the Indians caught him and my goodness wasn't he emborrassed!
And he was too Early-American to write for advice from Emily Post,
So he prepared to give up the ghost,
And he prayed a prayer but I don't know whether it was a silent one or a vocal one,
Because the Indians were going to dash his brains out and they weren't going to give him an anaesthetic, not even a local one,
But along came Pocahontas and she called off her father's savage minions,
Because she was one of the most prominent Virginians,
And her eyes went flash flash,
And she said, Scat, you po'red trash,
And she begged Captain John Smith's pardon,
And she took him for a walk in the gyarden,
And she said, Ah reckon ah sho' would have felt bad if anything had happened to you-all,

And she told him about her great-uncle Hiawatha and her
    cousin Sittin' Bull and her kissin' cousin King Philip,
    and I don't know who-all,
And he said You'd better not marry me, you'd better
    marry John Rolfe,
So he bade her farewell and went back to England which
    adjoins Scotland, where they invented golf.

BEAT THAT LIGHT!

I think the horses must be laughing,
Kicking up their heels and chaffing,
Watching from their green abode
The things that drove them off the road,
Whinnying in soft derision
At breakdown, blowout and collision,
Neighing, as they roam the prairies,
Motorists' obituaries.

Read the epitaphs on Monday
Of drivers various and Sunday;
Beep the horn and howl the klaxon
For Hebrew, Latin, and Anglo-Saxon;
Howling klaxon, beeping horn,
The funeral dirge of Monday morn,
Usher out the unlucky drivers
Without convincing the survivors.
Here's a curve and here's a truck,
Take a chance, and trust to luck;
The next one's practically standing still—
We'll pass it at the top of the hill.
That's the trick, you're doing fine;
Now try cutting out of line!
What of the surgeon and mortician
If drivers drove without ambition?

Every one-horse-power mind has bought
Its ninety-horse-power juggernaut
And rideth handsome, high and wide
In registered, licensed homicide,
Thus solving neatly throughout the nation
The problem of over-population
What is that sound that follows after?
The echo, my friend, of equine laughter.

BERNARR MACFADDEN

Bernarr Macfadden has given the preamble to the Constitution a sequel,

And established the fact that all women are created physiqual.

What is more, he has logically developed a little-known theory of Rousseau's;

Viz.: that there is a definite connection between fine torsos and fine trousseaux.

Yes, many a tenor or baritone has succumbed to some contralto or soprano

Who learned from Mr Macfadden about *mens sana in corpore sano.*

As a publisher he invariably puts his trust

In a picture of a hip or a bust.

Perhaps the idea was impromptu

But look what he has comptu!

He could now, if he wished, celebrate every Epiphany

By purchasing a fine solitaire diamond from Mr Tiffany;

Or again, if he so desired, he could buy for each of his friends on Septuagesima

A steel girder or turret from the works of Bessemer.

That's what the human body if properly exploited is capable of.

What is this thing called love?

IT ALL DEPENDS ON WHO YOU ARE

I am a kindly man at heart,
Awake to human needs,
A diligent student of the art
Of doing kindly deeds.
I never turn a beggar away
(And don't the beggars know it!)
And every night I quietly pray
To be a better poet.
Yet no reporter grasps his pen
To praise my noble nature,
But prefers perhaps infamouser men
Of famouser nomenclature.

There's Orson Welles,
And Stephen Early,
And the Dardanelles,
And General Hurley,
And Lucille Ball,
And Salvador Dali,
And people who call
Miss Parsons 'Lollie,'
And if these or others of the headline ilk
Give an overfed kitten a sip of milk,
The presses whirl
And the newsboys roar,
And the press has recorded one good deed more.

It all depends on who you are;
Yes indeed, you have said it, it's a fact;
Act kindly; but it's well to be a star,
If expecting any credit for the act.
It is sad,
But true,
That I
And you

Could spend our days in benevolent ways
And a damn would be given by nobody.
Nobody,
No, nobody.
We could guide old ladies across the street,
And stand old ladies to a bite to eat,
And give old ladies a lift to town,
And help old ladies knock the landlord down,
And a damn would be given by nobody.

I am, I've said, a kindly man,
Of less than modest wealth,
And I sometimes tire, as a person can,
Of doing good by stealth.
I frequently go without a meal
That an orphan may have his,
But the lonely inner glow I feel
My only guerdon is.
O, oft I've handed some hag in weeds
My final Camel or Tareyton,
But nobody chronicles the deeds
Of this Forgotten Samaritan.

But there's George Raft,
And Josef Stalin,
And Senator Taft,
And Gracie Allen,
And Mayor Hague,
And Annie Sheridan,
And Vera Vague,
And the Mayor of Meriden,
And if they or others in a similar pickle
Should bestow on the Aga Khan a nickel,
Watch the presses whirl
And the newsboys roar
As the press records one good deed more.

It all depends on who you are;
Yes indeedy, you have said it, it's the truth;
I'd be selfisher and happier by far
Had I learned that simple lesson in my youth.
For it's plain
To see
That you
And me
Could sit up nights over other people's plights,
And a damn would be given by nobody.
Nobody,
No, nobody.
You can rescue old men from the depths of gin
And restore old men to their long-lost kin
You can give old men the coats off your backs
And help old men evade the income tax,
But a damn will be given by nobody
Unless you're somebody.

THE PULPITEERS HAVE HAIRY EARS

There are too many people who think that just because
    they have parishes or dioceses
It imparts infallibility to all their biaseses.
Just give them a pulpit or two under their belts and they
    become very zealous
In forcing their opinions of everything on to everybody
    ealous.
I wonder why it is that so many clerics
Must be perpetually in hysterics.
It's odd, but at any hint of gaiety
On the part of the laity
Their furies and rages
Fill pages and pages and pages.
When the American girl was first by Mr Ziegfeld glorified
They were all violently horrified
And they gave vent to loud jeremiads
Over Mr White's amorous, clamorous dryads
And I hate to think what would happen if they should get
    a glimpse
Of one of Mr Carroll's charming undraped nimpse.
Yet I am sure none of those lovely girls has done anyone
    any harm,
For who is any the worse for a view of a shapely artistic
    feminine leg or arm?
Also clerics are very apt to become bitter at my, and
    bitter at your
Ideas of what is or is not proper in current literature.
Their speech is luxuriant
With words such as lewd, lascivious, obscene and prurient.
Don't they know that such a loud, nasty noise
Just puts ideas into the heads of little girls and boys?
Neither do clerics like prize-fighting, cock-fighting, bull-
    fighting or any other kind of fighting
Unless it is a war, in which case they urge people to go
    out and do a lot of smiting.

In fact the world is so full of a number of amusing things
That twenty-five per cent of its ministers seem to be as
  unhappy as ex-kings.
The other seventy-five per cent are very nice
But I wish we could dispose of the remainder in a trice
For I think that they are nothing but pulpiteers
And for them I give the opposite of three cheers.

INVOCATION

(SMOOT PLANS TARIFF BAN ON IMPROPER BOOKS — News Item)

Senator Smoot (Republican, Ut.)
Is planning a ban on smut.
Oh rooti-ti-toot for Smoot of Ut.
And his reverend occiput.
Smite, Smoot, smite for Ut.,
Grit your molars and do your dut.,
Gird up your l—ns,
Smite h—p and th—gh,
We'll all be Kansas
By and by.

Smite, Smoot, for the Watch and Ward,
For Hiram Johnson and Henry Ford,
For Bishop Cannon and John D., Junior,
For Governor Pinchot of Pennsylvunia,
For John S. Sumner and Elder Hays
And possibly Edward L. Bernays,
For Orville Poland and Ella Boole,
For Mother Machree and the Shelton pool.
When smut's to be smitten
Smoot will smite
For G—d, for country,
And Fahrenheit.

Senator Smoot is an institute
Not to be bribed with pelf;
He guards our homes from erotic tomes
By reading them all himself.
Smite, Smoot, smite for Ut.,
They're smuggling smut from Balt. to Butte!

Strongest and sternest
Of your s—x
Scatter the scoundrels
From Can. to Mex.!

Smite, Smoot, for Smedley Butler,
For any good man by the name of Cutler,
Smite for the W.C.T.U.,
For Rockne's team and for Leader's crew,
For Florence Coolidge and Admiral Byrd,
For Billy Sunday and John D., Third,
For Grantland Rice and for Albie Booth,
For the Woman's Auxiliary of Duluth,
Smite, Smoot,
Be rugged and rough,
Smut if smitten
Is front-page stuff.

IT'S ALWAYS APPLEBLOSSOM TIME,
UNFORTUNATELY

Dear friends, I am agitated because the world is so full of
a number of things that puzzle me,

And you are sadly mistaken if you think that any craven
fear of displaying my ignorance is going to muzzle me.

Now, if you take the way of a ship on the sea, or the way
of a man with a maid, or the way of an eagle,

And I can follow them like a beagle,

And I can also understand the way of Achilles with the
maidens and the way of Br'er Rabbit and Br'er Fox and
Br'er Possum,

But I will be the Burial of Sir John Moore at Corunna if I
understand the way of people who go around saying
they Would God they were a tender appleblossom.

As a rule I deprecate severity,

But I must say that when I hear anybody saying Would to
God they were a tender appleblossom I question their
sincerity.

In the first place if they were an appleblossom at all, why
to them it would be one

Whether they were tender or tough or rare or well done.

And one thing more:

What do they want to be any kind of appleblossom for?

Presumably they want to be an appleblossom because
they are in love, but appleblossoms never get to stand
up beside their beloved in church or chapel,

No, the most romantic thing that happens to appleblossoms is that once in a while they grow up to be an
apple,

So I'd like to know what the country is coming to and I
think we ought to discuss it,

Because I am afraid all the younger generation that used
to want to grow up to be a president or a movie star
or a fireman will now set their hearts on growing up
to be a pippin or a russet.

Loose talk is loose talk, whether it emanates from Washington or Palo Alto,

And somehow it seems even looser when it emanates from either a male or female contralto,

And loose talkers are something that we have more than ample of,

And I think it high time that some of them were made an example of,

So I certainly hope and pray

That sometime soon somebody will be in love with a handsome young neurologist and will say Would God they were a tender appleblossom and they will get their wish and turn into a tender appleblossom and then ripen into an apple and then keep the doctor away.

JUST A LEAF OF LETTUCE, AND SOME LEMON JUICE, THANK YOU

The human body is composed
Of head and limbs and torso,
Kept slim by gents
At great expense,
By ladies, even more so.

The human waistline will succumb
To such and such a diet.
The ladies gnaw
On carrots raw,
Their husbands will not try it.

The human bulk can be compressed
By intricate devices,
Which ladies hie
In droves to buy
At very highest prices.

The human shape can be controlled
By rolling on the floor.
Though many wives
Thus spend their lives,
To husbands it's a bore.

But human weight will also yield
To friendlier exercise;
A pleasing plan
That selfish Man
Upon the golf-course tries.

Though excess flesh can be removed,
We're told, by this and that,
You cannot win,
The thin stay thin,
The fat continue fat.

LOCUST-LOVERS, ATTENTION!

My attention has been recently focused
Upon the seventeen-year locust.
This is the year
When the seventeen-year locusts are here,
Which is the chief reason my attention has been focused
Upon the seventeen-year locust.
Overhead, underfoot, they abound,
And they have been seventeen years in the ground,
For seventeen years they were immune to politics and
    class war and capital taunts and labour taunts,
And now they have come out like billions of insect
    débutantes,
Because they think that after such a long wait,
Why they are entitled to a rich and handsome mate,
But like many another hopeful débutante they have been
    hoaxed and hocus-pocussed,
Because all they get is another seventeen-year locust.
Girl locusts don't make any noise,
But you ought to hear the boys.
Boy locusts don't eat, but it is very probable that they take a
    drink now and again, and not out of a spring or fountain,
Because they certainly do put their heads together in the
    treetops and render Sweet Adeline and She'll Be Comin'
    Round the Mountain.
I for one get bewildered and go all hot and cold
Every time I look at a locust and realize that it is seventeen
    years old;
It is as fantastic as something out of H. G. Wells or
    Jules Verne or G. A. Henty
To watch a creature that has been underground ever
    since it hatched shortly previous to 1920,
Because locusts also get bewildered and go hot and cold
    because they naturally expected to find Jess Willard
    still the champion,
And Nita Naldi the vampion,

And Woodrow Wilson on his way to Paris to promote
the perpetually not-yet-but-soon League,
And Washington under the thumb of Wayne B. Wheeler
and the Anti-Saloon League,
Indeed I saw one locust which reminded me of a god-
motherless Cinderella,
Because when it emerged from the ground it was whistling
Dardanella.
Dear locusts, my sympathy for you is intense,
Because by the time you get adjusted you will be defunct,
leaving nothing behind you but a lot of descendants
who in turn will be defunct just as they get adjusted
seventeen years hence.

LET GEORGE DO IT, IF YOU CAN FIND HIM

The wind comes walloping out of the West,
And the sky is lapis lazuli,
And the hills are bold in red and gold,
And I cannot take it casually.
Oh, cruel day for a man to spend
At counter or desk or forge!
I think I shall stray from duty today,
And turn it over to George.

George! George!   Where are you, George?
Clear the air for a call to George!
There is work to be done, dear George,
And fame to be won, dear George!
There are words to write,
And columns to add,
And everyone says
That George is the lad.
Here is a pen and here is a pencil,
Here's a typewriter, here's a stencil,
Here is a list of today's appointments,
And all the flies in all the ointments,
The daily woes that a man endures—
Take them, George, they're yours!

I will arise and roam the fields
Where edible coveys flutter,
I will conquer, methinks, the perilous links
With a true and deadly putter.
I'll forsake the grime of the city street
For valley and hill and gorge;
I will, or would, or I shall, or should,
But I can't get hold of George!

George! George!   Where are you, George?
Come out from under the sofa, George!
I thought you were braver, George!
I'm doing you a favour, George!
You can use my desk,
And sit in my chair,
Snugly away
From the nasty air.
Safe from the other fellow's habits,
Safe from returning without any rabbits,
Safe from treacherous spoons and brassies,
And the flaming shorts of the golfing lassies.
All this, dear George, I am trying to spare you.
George!   You slacker, where are you?

LINES TO A THREE-NAME LADY

Mrs Hattie Boomer Spink,
You puzzle me a lot.
Do you, I wonder, ever think?
And, if you do, of what?

Oh, solons bow like slender reeds
Beneath your firm resolve.
Your words I know, I know your deeds—
But whence do they evolve?

Do you employ a cerebrum,
And eke a cerebellum?
Or do you simply let 'em come,
With Gabriel at the hellum?

Nay, show me not your LL.D.
From Oklahoma Christian;
This honorary verdegree
Doth only beg the question.

Your native mental processes
Imply some secret canker;
Instead of thoughts, antipathies;
Instead of reason, rancour.

The ripple in your skull that spreads
From some primeval pebble,
How quickly washes o'er the heads
Of prophet and of rebel!

You three-name woman, Mrs Spink,
You puzzle me a lot.
Do you, I wonder, ever think?
And if you do, of what?

When gossip first began to link
Your name with that of Mr Spink,
O Hattie Boomer, did you think?
—And what's become of Mr Spink?

THE CARIBOU

Among the forests of the North,
The caribou walks back and forth.
The North is full of antlered game,
But none so pervious to fame.
For sportsmen who demand the best,
The caribou leads all the rest.
I hardly dare to tell you, madam,
I call him Caribou Ben Adhem.

THE STRANGE CASE OF MR BALLANTINE'S
VALENTINE

Once upon a time there was an attorney named Mr Ballantine.

He lived in the spacious gracious days of the nineteenth century

Mr Ballantine didn't know they were spacious and gracious

He thought they were terrible.

The reason he thought they were terrible was that love had passed him by.

Mr Ballantine had never received a valentine.

He said to his partner, My name is Mr Ballantine and I have never received a valentine.

His partner said, Well my name is Mr Bogardus and I have received plenty of valentines and I just as soon wouldn't.

He said Mr Ballantine didn't know when he was well off.

Mr Ballantine said, I know my heart, I know my mind, I know I long for a valentine.

He said here it was St Valentine's day and when he sat down at his desk what did he find?

Valentines?

No.

I find affidavits, said Mr Ballantine.

That's the kind of valentine I get, said Mr Ballantine.

Mr Bogardus said that affidavit was better than no bread.

Mr Ballantine said that affidavit, affidavit, affidavit onward, into the valley of death rode the six hundred.

Mr Bogardus said that any man who would rhyme 'onward' with 'six hundred' didn't deserve any affidavits at all.

Mr Ballantine said coldly that he was an attorney, not a poet, and Mr Bogardus had better take the matter up directly with Lord Tennyson.

Mr Bogardus said Oh, all right, and speaking of lords, he couldn't remember who was the king before David, but Solomon was the king affidavit.

Mr Ballantine buried Mr Bogardus in the cellar and went out in search of love.

Towards evening he encountered a maiden named Herculena, the Strongest Woman in the World.

He said, Madam, my name is Mr Ballantine and I have never received a valentine.

Herculena was delighted.

She said, My name is Herculena the Strongest Woman in the World, and I have never received a valentine either.

Mr Ballantine and Herculena decided to be each other's valentine.

All was merry as a marriage bell.

Mr Ballantine nearly burst with joy.

Herculena nearly burst with pride.

She flexed her biceps.

She asked Mr Ballantine to pinch her muscle.

Mr Ballantine recovered consciousness just in time to observe the vernal equinox.

He thought she said bustle.

THE STRANGE CASE OF MR DONNYBROOK'S
BOREDOM

Once upon a time there was a man named Mr Donnybrook.

He was married to a woman named Mrs Donnybrook.

Mr and Mrs Donnybrook dearly loved to be bored.

Sometimes they were bored at the ballet, other times at
the cinema.

They were bored riding elephants in India and elevators
in the Empire State Building.

They were bored in speakeasies during Prohibition and in
cocktail lounges after Repeal.

They were bored by Grand Dukes and garbagemen,
débutantes and demimondaines, opera singers and
operations.

They scoured the Five Continents and the Seven Seas in
their mad pursuit of boredom.

This went on for years and years.

One day Mr Donnybrook turned to Mrs Donnybrook.

My dear, he said, we have reached the end of our rope.

We have exhausted every yawn.

The world holds nothing more to jade our titillated
palates.

Well, said Mrs Donnybrook, we might try insomnia.

So they tried insomnia.

About two o'clock the next morning Mr Donnybrook said, My, insomnia is certainly quite boring, isn't it?

Mrs Donnybrook said it certainly was, wasn't it?

Mr Donnybrook said it certainly was.

Pretty soon he began to count sheep.

Mrs Donnybrook began to count sheep, too.

After awhile Mr Donnybrook said, Hey, you're counting my sheep!

Stop counting my sheep, said Mr Donnybrook.

Why, the very idea, said Mrs Donnybrook.

I guess I know my own sheep, don't I?

How? said Mr Donnybrook.

They're cattle, said Mrs Donnybrook.

They're cattle, and longhorns at that.

Furthermore, said Mrs Donnybrook, us cattle ranchers is shore tired o' you sheepmen plumb ruinin' our water.

I give yuh fair warnin', said Mrs Donnybrook, yuh better git them woolly Gila monsters o' yourn back across the Rio Grande afore mornin' or I'm a-goin' to string yuh up on the nearest cottonwood.

Carramba! sneered Mr Donnybrook. Thees ees free range, no?

No, said Mrs Donnybrook, not for sheep men.

She strung him up on the nearest cottonwood.

Mr Donnybrook had never been so bored in his life.

THE STRANGE CASE OF THE BLACKMAILING DOVE

Once upon a time there was a flock of doves.

They used to sit around the dovecote and coo.

The littlest dove was named Daingerfield.

Daingerfield could coo like the dickens, but he never got anything to eat.

Whenever anything to eat turned up, the buxom doves elbowed him out of the way.

The buxom doves got buxomer and buxomer.

Daingerfield got tenuouser and tenuouser.

Meanwhile he kept on cooing.

One day his mind was weakened by starvation and he forgot his lines.

He didn't say Coo.

He said Boo.

The buxom doves were panic-stricken. They fluttered around him like doves.

Daingerfield knows all, said the buxom doves. But good old Daingerfield won't tell, will you Daingerfield?

Boo, said Daingerfield.

Thenceforth the buxom doves presented the daintiest titbits to Daingerfield.

This is the life, he thought.

Boo, he said. Who's holding out on a titbit? Boo!

After a while the doves were invited to a society wedding.

It was the wedding of Felise Bankery, only child of Mrs Liz. Bankery Brokery Buttery and the late Reginald Bankery, the noted runner-up.

Felise was to marry the dashing Borogavian mixed triples runner-up, Baron Von Luciano.

Mrs Liz. Bankery Brokery Buttery thought a flock of doves in church would be nice.

Different, she said, and sort of symbolic.

The doves were released as the happy pair stood at the altar.

The cathedral echoed with their cooing.

Daingerfield couldn't see a thing. He sulked until the cooing stopped.

Boo! said Daingerfield clearly.

The bride jumped. So did the groom. Then they beckoned to Daingerfield.

This is soft, thought Daingerfield. He approached, booing mellifluously.

Why do you boo? asked Felise. Is it because of the brace and a half of twins ensuing from my secret marriage to the chauffeur?

Boo, said Daingerfield with a smirk.

Why do you boo? asked Baron Von Luciano. Is it because the social position of a baron in Borogavia is that of an extra waiter at a banquet?

Boo, said Daingerfield with another smirk.

The bride turned to the groom.

After all, she said simply, a baron is a baron, and we don't have to go to Borogavia, do we?

The groom turned to the bride.

After all, he said, a hundred million is a hundred million, and we can fire the chauffeur, can't we?

No indeed, said the bride.

Coo, said Daingerfield.

THE STRANGE CASE OF THE DEAD DIVORCEE

Once upon a time there was a beautiful woman named Mrs Geraldine McGregor Hamilton Garfinkle Boyce.

Her first husband Mr McGregor, divorced her for infidelity.

That wasn't his real reason but he didn't want to blast her reputation.

Her second husband, Mr Hamilton, divorced her for infidelity, too.

He had better grounds, which he was too chivalrous to mention.

Her third husband, Mr Garfinkle, was a cad.

He prepared a statement for the press setting forth his actual motives for divorcing her.

Her white-haired old mother pled tearfully with him for seven hours, pausing only to telephone her maid to bring over a dozen clean handkerchiefs.

Mr Garfinkle, if a cad, was a soft-hearted cad.

He destroyed his original damaging statement and informed the press that he was divorcing his wife for infidelity.

It was in June that Mrs Geraldine McGregor Hamilton Garfinkle became Mrs Geraldine McGregor Hamilton Garfinkle Boyce.

It was in July that Mr Boyce slaughtered her with a priceless heirloom, an ice-pick.

At the trial, Mr Boyce pled guilty.

She was infidelitous, said Mr Boyce, and I saw red.

Mr Boyce's lawyer asked him if he didn't have a better excuse.

Maybe I have, said Mr Boyce, but my lips are sealed.

De mortuis, you know, said Mr Boyce.

I will only say that she was infidelitous.

Mr Boyce was convicted and condemned to die.

Came Mr Boyce's Execution Eve.

The reporters were already strapping their cameras to their ankles when a delegation awaited upon the Governor.

The delegation consisted of Mr McGregor, Mr Hamilton, and Mr Garfinkle.

There are extenuating circumstances in the case of Mr Boyce, said Mr McGregor.

It is time the truth about Geraldine McGregor Hamilton Garfinkle Boyce were told, said Mr Hamilton.

I would have told it long ago but for my soft heart, said Mr Garfinkle.

Geraldine McGregor Hamilton Garfinkle Boyce was a juleper-in-the-manger, said Mr McGregor, Mr Hamilton, and Mr Garfinkle.

She never drank but half a mint julep, they said.

But when she was offered a mint julep, did she quietly drink half of it and quietly give the other half to her husband when he had finished his?

Not Geraldine McGregor Hamilton Garfinkle Boyce! they said.

She said no thank you, I only want half of one, I'll drink half of my husband's, they said.

Other women's husbands get a julep and a half, they said.

Geraldine McGregor Hamilton Garfinkle Boyce's husbands get half a julep, they said.

The Governor pardoned Mr Boyce forthwith.

Ten minutes later the Governor's butler discovered the body of the Governor's lady on the veranda.

The ice-pick that protruded from her heart was a priceless heirloom.

THE STRANGE CASE OF THE PLEASING TAXI-
DRIVER

Once upon a time there was a taxi-driver named Llewellyn Abdullah—White—Male—5-10½—170.

Llewellyn had promised his mother he would be the best
taxi-driver in the world.

His mother was in Heaven.

At least, she was in a Fool's Paradise because her boy was
the best taxi-driver in the world.

He was, too.

He called his male passengers Sir instead of Mac, and his
female passengers Madam instead of Sister.

On rainy nights his flag was always up.

He knew not only how to find the Waldorf, but the
shortest route to 5954 Gorsuch Avenue.

He said Thank you when tipped, and always had change
for five dollars.

He never drove with a cigar in his mouth, lighted or un-
lighted.

If you asked him to please not drive so fast, he drove not
so fast, and didn't get mad about it, either.

He simply adored traffic cops, and he was polite to Sunday
drivers.

When he drove a couple through the park he never looked
back and he never eavesdropped.

My boy is the best taxi-driver in the world and no eaves-dropper, said his mother.

The only trouble was that the bad taxi-drivers got all the business.

Llewellyn shrank from White—Male—5-$10\frac{1}{2}$—170 to Sallow—Male—5-$9\frac{3}{4}$—135.

Cheest, Llewellyn, said his mother.

Cheest, Mother, replied Llewellyn.

Llewellyn and his mother understood each other.

He took his last five dollars in dimes and nickles which he had been saving for change and spent it on cigars at two for a nickel.

The next day he insulted seven passengers and a traffic cop, tore the fender off a car from Enid, Oklahoma, and passed through 125th Street while taking a dear old lady from 52nd to 58th.

That evening he had forty dollars on the clock.

Llewellyn is no longer the best taxi-driver in the world, but his licence reads White—Male—5-11—235.

In the park he is the father of all eavesdroppers.

Couples who protest find him adamant.

Since he is the father of all eavesdroppers and adamant, I think we might call him an Adam-ant-Evesdropper and there leave him.

Good-bye, Llewellyn.

129

THE STRANGE CASE OF THE TSAR'S SUPERIORITY COMPLEX

Once upon a time there was a Balkan state.

The name of the State was Bulgonia.

Bulgonia was ruled by a Tsar.

The name of the Tsar was Borealis.

He was known as Tsar Borealis of Bulgonia because his name was Borealis and he was the Tsar of Bulgonia.

Tsar Borealis was very democratic.

You may think it difficult for a Tsar to be democratic.

It isn't.

If a postman gets a cold, it's unfortunate.

If a Tsar gets a cold, it's democratic.

If a bookkeeper wheels his baby around the block, it's Astoria.

If a Tsar wheels his baby around the block, it's practically Communistic.

If a concierge says he admires American institutions, it's untrue.

If a Tsar says he admires American institutions it's a sign that somebody wants to float a loan.

Tsar Borealis got colds and wheeled his baby around block after block and simply adored American institutions.

He was a one-hundred-per-cent democrat.

When an American is a one-hundred-per-cent democrat he gets in wrong with his wife.

When a Tsar is a one-hundred-per-cent democrat he gets in the papers.

Tsar Borealis's press clippings from New York and Washington alone were practically pushing him out of the palace.

Sofia, so good.

Unfortunately, Tsar Borealis asked his Prime Minister one day what was the source of sleeping sickness.

The Prime Minister told him the tse-tse fly.

Tsar Borealis said the Prime Minister meant the tse fly.

The Prime Minister begged His Imperial Highness's pardon, but said he meant the tse-tse fly.

Tsar Borealis wouldn't believe it until he saw it in the dictionary.

Then he was furious.

He said democrat or no democrat he wasn't going to be out-hyphenated by any African fly.

He said that from now on he was the Tsar-tsar Borealis. and everybody had better look out.

The Tsar-tsar moved at once to Walla Walla.

He refused to wear any garment but a lava-lava.

I regret to state that it was not long before he perished.

But he met the end smiling.

The ailment was beri-beri.

ALLERGY MET A BEAR

I heard them speak of allergy,
I asked them to explain,
Which when they did, I asked them
To please explain again.

I found the pith of allergy
In Bromides tried and true;
For instance, you like lobster,
But lobster don't like you.

Does aspirin cause your eyes to cross?
Do rose-leaves make you nervy?
Do old canaries give you boils?
Do kittens give you scurvy?

Whatever turns your skin to scum,
Or turns your blood to glue,
Why, that's the what, the special what,
That you're allergic to.

O allergy, sweet allergy,
Thou lovely word to me!
Swift as an heiress Reno-bound
I called on my M.D.

This doctor was obliged to me
For reasons I must edit.
(I knew he had two extra wives,
And neither did him credit.)

I spoke to him of allergy;
Perhaps I clenched my fist;
But when I left his domicile
I had a little list.

I can't attend the opera now,
Or sleep within a tent;
I cannot ride in rumble seats;
My allergies prevent.

Oh, garden parties speed my pulse,
And pound my frame to bits;
I'd mind the child on Thursdays,
But children give me fits.

When Duty sounds her battlecry,
Say never that I shirk;
It isn't laziness at all,
But an allergy to work.

Love is a word that is constantly heard,
Hate is a word that's not.
Love, I am told, is more precious than gold,
Love, I have read, is hot.
But hate is the verb that to me is superb,
And love is a drug on the mart.
Any kiddie in school can love like a fool,
But hating, my boy, is an art.

OH—
You and I and many others
Love our sweethearts and our mothers,
Love our spouses, love our tots,
Ship our love in carload lots—
Parsley, parsnips, beginner's luck,
Yorkshire pudding, Bombay Duck,
Sunup, sundown, sunray lamps,
Sporting prints or postage stamps,
Persimmons, even good persimmons,
Lifted faces, fallen womens—
Not a topic named above
That countless millions do not love.
Something somewhere's bound to pop.
I for one suggest we stop.

Hate is a word that is constantly slurred,
Love is the word that's lauded.
Hate, people say, is completely *passé*,
Vulgar, my dear, and saudid.
The atmosphere swoons with amorous tunes,
Like turtle dove calling to dove.
We are fairly discreet about what we eat,
But gosh! are we gluttons in love!

OH—
Fellow countrymen and others,
Turn, I beg, upon your mothers.
No more nonsense from the vicar—
He will only make you sicker.
Learn, before it grows too late,
Fellow countrymen, to hate.
Learn to hate banana salads,
Travel films and cowboy ballads,
Literati, early risers,
Politicians, advertisers,
Fruit-juice cocktails, borrowed wit,
Ladies who rely on IT;
And fall, I pray, on every crooner,
Stuff his mouth with goona-goona.
Develop all your latent phobias,
And heaven's blessings will be copious.

IT'S SNUG TO BE SMUG

Oh, sometimes I wish I had the wings of an angel because then I could fly through the air with the greatest of ease,

And if I wanted to be somewhere else I could get there without spending any money on taxis or railroad tickets or tips or fees,

Yes, I could fly to Paris and do as a Parisian, or fly to Rome and do as a Roman,

But on the other hand wings would necessitate my sleeping on my abdomen,

So I don't really wish I had the wings of an angel, but sometimes I wish I had the sweet voice of a thrush,

And then if I sang an Indian Love Lyric why thousands of beautiful beauties would hearken and quiver and blush,

And it would be a treat to hear my rendition of Sweet Alice Ben Bolt,

But on the other hand who would go to hearken to anybody who was known to eat insects and moult?

So I don't really wish I had the sweet voice of a thrush, but sometimes I wish I had the courage of a lion,

And then I could look life in the eye with a will of iron,

And to a goose, or a burglar, or even a butler, I wouldn't hesitate to say Boo!

But on the other hand I might encounter a goose or a burglar or a butler who had the courage of a lion too,

So I don't really wish I had the courage of a lion but sometimes I wish I had an elephant's muscle,

And then when somebody fainted or got run over I could always get in the front of spectators no matter how thick the hustle and bustle,

But on the other hand I would probably find myself in some job where such strength would be utilitarian,

So if I had the muscle of an elephant, why instead of lying back comfortably and wishing I had the muscle of an elephant, why I would probably be busy building a tower in Manhattan or tunnelling through a peak in Darian,

So I don't really wish I had the muscle of an elephant but sometimes I wish I had the innocence of a lamb,

And then I would never wake up crying Fie on me!   What an un-innocent sinner I am!

But on the other hand innocence is a security on which it is hard to borrow,

Because all it means is that either you get eaten by a wolf today or else the shepherd saves you from the wolf so he can sell you to the butcher tomorrow,

So I do not really wish I had the innocence of a lamb,

I guess I'll stay just as I am.

LINES TO BE SCRIBBLED ON SOMEBODY
ELSE'S THIRTIETH MILESTONE

Thirty today?   Cheer up, my lad!
The good old thirties aren't so bad.
Life doesn't end at twenty-nine,
So come on in, the water's fine.
I, too, when thirty crossed my path,
Turned ugly colours with shame and wrath.
I kicked, I scratched, I bit my nails,
I indulged in tantrums the size of whales,
I found it hard to forgive my mater
For not having had me ten years later.
I struggled with reluctant feet
Where dotage and abdomens meet.
Like the tongue that seeks the missing tooth
I yearned for my extracted youth.
Since then some years have ambled by
And who so satisfied as I.
The thirties are things I wallow among,
With naught but pity for the young.
The less long ago that people were born
The more I gaze on them with scorn,
And each Thanksgiving I Thanksgive
That I'm slowly learning how to live.
So conquer, boy, your grief and rage,
And welcome to the perfect age!
I hope good fairies your footsteps haunt,
And bring you everything you want,
From cowboy suits and Boy Scout knives,
To beautiful, generous, wealthy wives.
If you play the horses, may you play good horses,
If you want divorces, may you get divorces,

Be it plenty of sleep, or fortune, or fame,
Or to carry the ball for Notre Dame,
Whatever it is you desire or covet,
My boy, I hope you get it and love it.
And you'll use it a great deal better, I know,
Than the child that you were a day ago.

The world is much, much too full of a man whose name is
 legion,
And he gives me for one a pain in the cervical region.
This human hellgramite that I think we could all dispense
 with,
Is he who in every pleasant mixed gathering insists on
 dragging in the kind of anecdote that should, if em-
 ployed, be employed only to entertain gents with.
As a rule, when he is among his fellow men he is meek
 as a mouse,
But just watch him when there are three or four ladies,
 preferably sensitive, in the house.
It is on such an occasion
That he elects to be most rabidly Rabelaisian.
His persiflage would embarrass
The late Frank Harris,
And as you watch him scintillating
You have an overwhelming conviction that the room
 needs vintilating.
It isn't that you yourself have never guffawed
At humour that is, to put it mildly, broad,
Or consider yourself too nice
To indulge once in a while in a bit of risquéting on thin ice;
It's just that under the circumstances the mildew that
 passes for wit with this weevil
Happens to throw your digestive system into a revulsive
 upheaval.
Sometimes he fancies himself as a Lothario,
And other times as the principal comedian of a side-
 splitting obscenario,
But if you chance to grow restive
As his quips and cranks and wanton wiles get continually
 more suggestive,
And venture the opinion that a trip to the laundry
Could hardly fail to benefit some of the *double entendry*,

He will retort that his intentions and his remarks are all
    irreproachably refined,

And that if you see something wrong about them it only
    proves conclusively that you have a vulgar mind.

So after that, everybody is on the spot

And nobody knows whether to laugh or not,

And the evening gets more and more uncomfortable and
    at the same time duller and duller

As every few minutes he trots out a horse of another
    off-colour,

This I believe is his way of demonstrating that he is
    Sophisticated and not Provincial,

And if some good sophisticated gangster took him for a
    good sophisticated ride I should consider it nothing
    less than Providintial.

TWO SONGS FOR A BOSS NAMED
MR LONGWELL

Put it there, Mr Longwell, put it there!
You're a bear, Mr Longwell, you're a bear!
It's our verdict
That your service is perfect.
You're a regular American crusader
And you'll lick old H. L. Mencken's Armada.
You know life isn't all a picnic
But it hasn't made you a cynic.
From first to last
As the banner goes past
We'll sing our favourite air.
Our choice always narrows
To the man you can't embarrass,
So put it there, Mr Longwell, put it there!

II

L for loyalty to his grand old firm,
O for his eyes of blue,
N for his ideals and his spirit of co-operation,
G for his influence on me and you.
W for his ability to collect and co-ordinate facts,
E-L-L for the labour-saving card-index system he put
    through.
Put them all together, they spell LONGWELL,
Which is about what you might expect them to do.

POOR MR STRAWBRIDGE

Once there was a man named Mr Strawbridge,
And all he wanted was a drawbridge,
But when people asked him what kind
He couldn't make up his mind.
His fingernails he would bite and his thumbs he would
    twiddle
Trying to decide whether he wanted one that revolved on
    a pivot or one that went up in the middle,
So finally everybody went to Mr Strawbridge
And asked him why he wanted a drawbridge.
And Mr Strawbridge smiled a smile seraphic
And said he wanted it because he wanted to interfere
    with traffic.
He said that on his house he had a veranda built,
And it was comfortable enough for a Vanderbilt,
And he said it gave him great satisfaction
To sit on his veranda and watch the Atlantic Ocean in
    action
But he said sometimes on Sundays and holidays he
    couldn't see the Atlantic for the motorists,
And he said he'd rather see the former than the latter even
    though they were handsome and respectable Kiwanians
    and Lions and Rotarists,
And he said maybe he was a silly old goose,
But it always gave him a pain to see a line of automobiles
    practically hooked up together like freight cars on a
    long freight train, particularly when the freight train
    was ten miles long and you never seemed to get to the
    caboose,
And he said that doubtless all that gipsying was most
    romantic,
But he still preferred looking at the Atlantic
And he said he didn't see why people went out in one
    automobile between a lot of other automobiles, be-
    cause they didn't get any air or scenery,

No, they just got a view of the licence plate in front and a
  lot of annoyance and dust and gasolinery,
And therefore, said Mr Strawbridge,
Everybody else would see just as much and I would see
  much more if they were all held up somewhere by an
  open drawbridge,
So all his friends said he was a genius,
And they gave him a lot of orchids and gardenius,
But they never gave him a drawbridge,
And that is why I call him poor Mr Strawbridge.

LADIES' DAY

Women still excel as mothers,
Women still excel as wives,
Women still, in spite of diets,
Lead with forks and knives.
Women have the fairest faces,
Women have the softest hearts,
Women gain the greenest laurels
When they woo the arts.
Let me add to this preamble,
Women, women shouldn't gamble.

Yip! Whoop! Boop-boop-a-doop!
The frenzied treble rises,
The welkin reels to soprano squeals
When ladies win the prizes.
Fret! Fume! Grim, glum gloom!
Oh, what a crooked bank!
Clear the path for righteous wrath
When the ladies draw a blank.
Oh, girls will gamble if they choose,
But they shouldn't win and they shouldn't lose.

Women! First in intuition!
Lovely woman! Still untaught
That every time somebody wins,
Someone else is caught.
Women! Hers the sweetest accent
Heard on this terrestrial stage—
But not when raised in yelps of triumph,
Not when hoarse with rage.
That woman most is worth escorting
Who never, never goes a-sporting.

Bliss! Joy! Boy, oh boy!
She won through personal merit;
The tip came through, the dream came true,
The rabbit bit the ferret.
Boo! Shame! the world's to blame!
The cards were stacked agin her!
Rise, Huey, rise, some game devise
With every lady a winner.
Nevertheless, the girl I choose
Will never win and never lose.

SIGMUND FREUD

Who's afreud of the big bad dream?
Things are never what they seem;
Daddy's bowler, Auntie's thimbles,
Actually are shocking symbols.
Still, I think, a pig's a pig—
Ah, there, symbol-minded Sig!

THE FRIENDLY TOUCH

You go into a store and select half a dozen shirts and
  charge them,
And finally you get them paid for along about the time
  you either have to give them away or enlarge them,
And you don't go back to the store because although it
  has nice shirts, still, for your modest budget it's rather
  expensive,
And the possibilities of a charge account are too extensive,
You need some more shirts,
But your conscience hurts;
Your bureau drawer is emptied
But you refuse to be tempted;
You say, No, they have nice shirts but they look on any
  purchase under two hundred dollars with boredom,
And I simply can't afforedom.
Well, everything is simply splendid,
And suddenly you get a letter from them saying they have
  been looking over their accounts and note that they
  have not served you since April 15th, 1931, and in
  what way have they offended?
This is followed by other letters even more imploring,
Indeed the tone becomes positively adoring;
They beg you to purchase something from them,
They egg you to purchase something from them;
They hint that if their plea you ignore,
Why, they will simply close up their store,
And you succumb to their appealings,
And buy half a dozen shirts just so as not to hurt their
  feelings.
Well, their feelings seem to recover all right from the
  wreck,
Because about the middle of the following month you get
  a letter from them saying they have been looking over
  their accounts and how about favouring them with a
  cheque?

This is followed by other letters even more suggestive of
   lovers' meetings ending in journeys,
And in about two weeks they turn over their share of the
   correspondence to their attorneys,
So you send the cheque and the affair is ended,
And you swear off and in about a year you get a letter
   from them saying they have been looking over their
   accounts and note that they have not served you since
   October 2nd, 1936, and in what way have they offended?
Some people chase their own coat-tails in revolving doors,
And other people write letters for stores.

THE INSECT

The insect serves some useful end,
But what it is I've never kenned.
I do not like the ones that buzz,
I do not know a soul who does;
And as for those that crawl and creep,
The more they die, the less I weep.
Yet such is ego, low and high,
They'd rather be themselves than I.

THE INTRODUCTION

This is Mr Woolley, Mrs Nixon;
This is Mrs Nixon, Mr Woolley;
Mr Woolley, Mrs Nixon is a vixen;
Mrs Nixon, Mr Woolley is a bully.
Shake hands with Mr Woolley, Mrs Nixon;
Shake hands with Mrs Nixon, Mr Woolley;
And let the welkin shout that it's I who brought about
The meeting of the vixen and the bully.

Mrs Nixon is one of those ladies
With a disposition acquired in Hades.
What! you exclaim.   That placid blonde?
She's as shallow and calm as a lily pond!
I've seen her at parties, at dances, at teas,
Her crossest command is, If you please.
Well, give her a racket and bulging shorts
And put her out on the tennis courts;
Then, if you care to behold your vixen,
Give her for partner Mr Nixon.
Hark to her shrill and furious cries
As she damns his hands and feet and eyes.
It's mine! she shrieks.   She swings and misses.
Why didn't you get it, you swine? she hisses.
She explains to the world her vagrant serves;
Her clumsy partner upsets her nerves.
He scores a placement.   Says she, A miracle!
He doesn't.   She rocks with mirth hysterical.
Over the backstop, into the net
She angrily lollops game and set,
And sweetly barks, when the match is through,
We're beaten again, dear, thanks to you.

Mr Woolley, oh Mr Woolley!
Hell will welcome him warmly, fully.
What! you exclaim.   That genial fellow?
He's a chivalrous gentleman, mild and mellow.

Around the club, from lip to lip,
Run tales of his generous sportsmanship.
Well, if your stomach is strong and able,
Set him down at a contract table;
Then, if you care to behold your bully,
Give him for partner Mrs Woolley.
She should have bid, or she shouldn't have bid,
She shouldn't have done whatever she did.
Does she hold a hand? He bids it away;
He'd rather go down than let her play.
A celluloid duck, he loudly avers,
Might boast of better brains than hers.
And oft, with polished wit sardonic,
He hails her as poison, or Bubonic,
Or else with humour gay and easy,
Hopes she's enjoying her parcheesi.
He roars, with the last lost rubber concluded;
We've lost ten dollars, and that's what you did.

Oh, this is Mrs Woolley, Mr Nixon,
And this is Mr Nixon, Mrs Woolley;
Mr Woolley, Mrs Nixon is a vixen;
Mrs Nixon, Mr Woolley is a bully.
Shake hands with Mrs Woolley, Mr Nixon;
Shake hands with Mr Nixon, Mrs Woolley;
To both of you more power, and may your meeting
    flower
In the slaughter of a vixen and a bully.

RECIPE FOR A DICTATORSHIP

First catch your country,
Which is not so difficult for a demagogue of sufficient
  ruthlessness, plausibility, and effrontery,
But if you catch it by war or revolution debilitated,
Your task will be facilitated.
Its neck is what you place your foot upon,
And then you tell it that by every other nation in the
  world it is put upon,
And you wear some kind of childish raw head and bloody
  bones uniform because you wouldn't be a dictator if
  you weren't a good showman,
And you keep repeating that your people are hemmed in
  by a steel ring of predatory foemen,
And as there is really lots of room for everybody in your
  country because there aren't so many people in it as
  there were before the war,
Why, you shout that there aren't enough people to defend
  the country from its evil neighbours and you command
  all patriotic citizens to have a lot more,
And you offer prizes for triplets and twins,
And the race begins,
And the birthrate leaps like a startled fawn,
And you urge it on and on and on,
The cry is breed! breed!
Breed with speed!
The big bad enemy is at the gate,
Breed for the state!
So every hut produces its enormous family,
And you go around and pat the children on the head and
  the fathers on the back and smile a big smile with your
  teeth all glistening and enamelly,
And pretty soon you have your country populated as full
  as the Bronx Express during the rush hour and you say
  My gracious me!

What a wonderful, progressive, up-and-coming, expand-
ing nation we are!
We'll have to take over somebody else's country because
in our own country there isn't room for us,
And everybody in the League of Nations is a rotten egg
if they don't say Rah rah siss boom for us!
So then you go out to take over somebody else's nation,
And that takes care of your surplus population,
So then you find you haven't got as many people in your
country as your ambitions need,
So you inform your people again that they had better
hurry up and breed,
Which maybe they don't and maybe they do,
And again maybe, dear dictator, they begin to cogitate
about you.

SPECULATIVE REFLECTION

I wonder if the citizens of New York will ever get sufficiently wroth
To remember that Tammany cooks spoil the broth.

THE LOST CAUSE

There is nothing like a rousing slogan
For releasing necks from a tyrant's brogan;
Victory blooms from latent rout
At the lilt of a leader's well-phrased shout;
Dying men will forget to die
And obey a catchy battlecry.
Indeed, you may sway the swirling crowd
With any order sufficiently loud;
You may break a kingdom and gain a crown,
But you cannot make a crowd sit down.

O, down in front! Down in front!
The people behind implore.
There are giants to right and giants to left,
And Siamese giants before.
A halfback wriggles through the line,
A tackle blocks a punt,
The stadium rocks to thrills and shocks
And the cry of Down in front!
Sit down, sit down, the game grows frantic!
But the giants only grow more gigantic.

You people in front can see already;
You're sitting pretty; why not sit steady?
It's the people in front who stand up first,
And then expand till you hope they burst.
The people in front are all colossuses
With the bulk and also the hide of rhinocuses.
The little people sit behind;
They meekly and weakly go it blind,
Till at last they rise in brash defiance,
And what do you know? They too are giants!

O, down in front! Down in front!
The age-old slogan rings,
But the human elephants rise to their feet
As the desperate slugger swings.
The pitcher waves the fielders back,
The runners shuffle and shunt,
And fans who seethe and fail to breathe
Must yet cry Down in front!
Sit down, sit down, and a happy landing!
And all the elephants keep on standing.

THE NAME IS TOO FAMILIAR

You go away for a trip, either business or pleasure

And you think to settle down to a little anonymous leisure,

And the first thing you see on the train is a sign bearing the name of the porter,

And his name is Lafcadio Pauncefoote so you can't call him Boy or George, which eventually worries you into giving him an extra quarter,

And you go into the dining car a little later,

And there you are confronted with signs confiding to you the names of the steward and the waiter,

And the steward hovers over you like a hospitable owl,

And you can't call him Steward because now you think of him as Mr Feeney your host, so when he asks you how your steak is you say Splendid instead of Foul,

And you get off the train and into a taxi,

And there's a picture to tell you that the driver's name is Maxie,

And you don't want to be hemmed in by names, you want to be alone,

But you think, At least it's other people's names that are hounding me and not my own,

And you go and register at an hotel and up comes the third assistant manager with a third assistant managerial gurgle,

And he looks at the register and then shakes hands and says We're mighty glad to have you with us, Mr Alf B. Murgle,

We certainly hope you enjoy your stay, Mr Murgle,

And the bellboy gets the idea and says Right this way, Mr. Murgle,

And the elevator boy gets the idea and says This is your floor, Mr Murgle,

And the floor clerk gets the idea and says Good morning Mr Murgle, there's your door, Mr Murgle,

And the telephone girl gets the idea and says, Good
　morning Mr Murgle, okay Plaza 3-8362, Mr Murgle,
And the waiter gets the idea and says Will that be all, Mr
　Murgle? Thank you, Mr Murgle,
So your private life in the hotel is about as private as the
　private life of the Dionnes, but at first you are slightly
　flattered because you think Somebody important must
　have sent them word of you,
And after they have Mr Murgled you for the thousandth
　time you try to cash a two-dollar cheque and you dis-
　cover they have never heard of you,
Yes, it's all a figure of speech,
Because they not only know you, but also don't know
　you, and combine the worst features of each.
That's the beauty about a name, whenever we want to
　anonymously relax it pops up and prevents us,
And it is certainly nice to get home again and settle
　down as an obscure statistic in the census.

THE MAN WITH TWO NEW SUITS

Who is that well-dressed, handsome man?
Is everybody's eager cry,
I make response, for the fleeting nonce;
Excuse me, it is I!
The clangorous bells their homage pay,
The jubilant whistle toots,
And the murmur grows, Look, there he goes!
The man with two new suits!

The first is a tasteful quiet grey,
The second a quiet brown;
One wouldn't suppose such reticent clothes
Would so excite the town.
The coats display no waspish waist,
The trousers boast no pleats,
But the collars fit like Glyn and It,
And oh, the lordly seats!

On the gleaming steps of the Mansion House
The Mayor takes his stand
With welcoming teeth, and a laurel wreath
And a gold key in his hand.
The city is yours, the Mayor cries,
And the guard of honour salutes,
And the gaping crowd cheers long and loud
For the man with two new suits.

The brown one has a single breast,
And the breast of the grey is double,
And they mould the form to the perfect norm
Where the scapulae cease to trouble.
The trousers nestle round the hips,
Then flow like a weeping willow—
Oh, as gay am I as a butterfly,
Yet snug as the armadillo!

Who is that well-dressed handsome man?
The curious whispers mount;
Sir Gladwyn Jebb? or Clifton Webb?
Or Barbara's dapper Count?
Oh peace, my friends, and cease, my friends,
Your middle-class disputes;
It's I you see, it's me, it's me,
The man with two new suits.

The old suit bagged across the knees,
And it also bagged behind;
The foraging moth had pierced its cloth,
And the nap was neatly shined.
I gave that suit to a shabby tramp,
I thought his poverty earned it,
And he said, 'What's that?' And then he spat,
And he took it out and burned it.

But now bring forth your noblest malt,
Your noblest barley and grape,
Triumphal parade and cavalcade
And torrent of streamer tape!
Now man and child shall work no more,
But seize your zithers and lutes
And spend their days in endless praise
Of the man with two new suits!

THE SONG OF SONGS

Is anybody here in favour of a redistribution of wealth?

Because I think it ought to be redistributed, only not by force or by stealth,

Because it is only when other people have it and you haven't that it is evil,

So we had better try to correct the situation before it is made worse by a revolution or an upheaval.

Let us not be like the Soviets and fall prey to any communistic demagog,

No, surely we have more sense than a mujik and would yawn at arguments that keep them agog;

And let us not be sheep like a Fascist audience

Who get played on by their leaders like concertinas or accaudience;

Let us rather correct in our own 100% American way the wrongs that annoy and disgust us,

And correct them so the corrections will not offend the Constitution and Mr Hughes, our imposing Chief Justice;

Let us handle it in the manner of Washington and Jefferson and Jackson

And keep very level-headed and Anglo-Saxon.

There are several things standing in the way of a natural distribution of wealth, but if you want to know which is the chief thing, well, I will tell you which:

The rich marry only the rich.

It is one of our national disasters

That, broadly speaking, Astors and Vanderbilts and Rockefellers and Morgans never marry anybody but Morgans and Rockefellers and Vanderbilts and Astors,

Whereas if they only bestowed their affections on somebody in a lower crust,

Why money would be distributed over this broad land of ours like dust,

So I think they may all be rich but honest,

But I think their matchmaking proclivities ought to be harnessed.

Yes, if money marrying money were prohibited,

How speedily and how painlessly it would be redistributed.

Yes, yes, the rich and the poor can settle and forget their differences just as the Blue and the Grey have

As soon as we have a law saying that people can only marry people who have a lot less money than they have,

And that will be the end of all your present and future Townsends and Coughlins and Longs,

And that is why I call this piece the Song of Songs.

LET'S NOT GO TO THE THEATRE TONIGHT
or
WE COULDN'T GET SEATS ANYHOW

Light the lights at four o'clock, pull the curtains down,
Turn the radiator on, winter walks the town.
The speculators waken, and the critics are unloosed,
And all the summer theatres are coming home to roost.
For the drama has departed from Ogunquit,
The audience has vanished from Wiscasset,
And instead of city strangers
There is hay among the mangers
Of Skowhegan, and Carmel, and Cohasset.
Oh, when is a barn not a barn?
Riddle me this, I pray.
Why, not from about the middle of June
Till after Labour Day.
The evicted cows in the rain must browse
Till after Labour Day.

Order dinner early, dear, and robe yourself in style
As I telephone the broker for a couple on the aisle,
But hear the broker chuckle as he warbles like a finch,
There's nothing left but standing room, at eleven dollars
    an inch.
For the natives swarm upon us from Nantucket,
They throng from Painted Post and Triple Fork,
They've abandoned Martha's Vineyard
For Manhattan's fertile sin yard,
They are going to the theatre in New York.
Oh, when is a theatre not a theatre?
This is my wistful tune.
Why, not from after October first
Till around the middle of June.
You can't sit down at a play in town
Till around the middle of June.

So pack your evening gown away, unwave your wavèd
  hair,
No need to brave the traffic of Mr Times's Square.
The show we cannot see tonight for money or for love
Will adorn our local silo after June the middle of.
Then it's Ho! for Shaw and Shakespeare in Ogunquit,
And Connelly and Kaufman in Wiscasset!
We will take our Sidney Howard,
Our Maugham and Noel Coward,
In comfort, and Skowhegan, and Cohasset.
Oh, when is a play not a play?
And if it be thus, how be it?
Well, it's my belief that it's not a play
If you can't get in to see it.
So suppose we wait for a summer date,
And sit in a barn to see it.

THE ROOSTER

The rooster has a soul more bellicose
Than all your Ludendorffs and Jellicoes.
His step is prouder than Davy Crockett's,
As he swaggers by with his hands in his pockets.

THE SAGE OF DARIEN

Upon a peak in Darien
The Sage surveys his fellow men,
Exerting to its full capacity
His preternatural sagacity.
Sore eyes and empty stomach mutiny;
The Sage confines himself to scrutiny,
Occasionally sniffing through a tube
The vapour of a bouillon cube.
Thus, all his grosser instincts chastening,
He thinks to bring the vision hastening.
The truth about his fellow men,
He hopes, will bloom within his ken.
At last appears a tiny truth,
A sliver like a baby's tooth.
Now fast it grows, it swells, it waxes,
It multiplies itself like taxes.
The ultimate truth, for what it's worth,
Crowds minor truthlets off the earth.
The Sage cries Bother! through his beard;
Says he, Exactly what I feared.
I needn't have come to Darien
To scrutinize my fellow men;
It seems I've scaled this natural steeple
To learn what I've always known about people;
To confirm through sacrifice intense
The fact that people have no sense.
People are born in pain and woe,
In woe and pain through life they go,
Harpies attend their to-and-froing,
And yet the blockheads keep on going.
Dictators tread upon their necks,
And presidents their purses vex,
Republics rob them, monarchies milk them,
Revolutions unfailingly bilk them;
Tyrants imprison them and slaughter them;

Promoters take their stocks and water them;
Statements and bills pile high around them;
Sheriffs and credit departments hound them;
By ten-ton trucks they are forced from the roads;
Every October they change their abodes;
Frequent expensive diseases smite them;
Sunbeams burn them, mosquitoes bite them;
Employers jeer at their shiny diplomas;
Advertisers insult their aromas;
People are born in pain and woe,
In woe and pain through life they go;
They have no cause at all for thanksgiving,
And yet the idiots keep on living.
Upon a peak in Darien
The Sage renounced his fellow men.
His fellow men he did renounce,
And leapt, and lit, and didn't bounce.

THE VERY UNCLUBBABLE MAN

I observe, as I hold my lonely course,
That nothing exists without a source.
Thus, oaks from acorns, lions from cubs,
And health and wealth from the proper clubs.
There are yacht clubs, golf clubs, clubs for luncheon,
Clubs for flowing bowl and puncheon,
Clubs for dancing, clubs for gambling,
Clubs for sociable Sunday ambling,
Clubs for inbibing literature,
And clubs for keeping the cinema pure,
Clubs for friendship, clubs for snobbery,
Clubs for smooth political jobbery.
As civilization onward reels,
It's clubs that grease the speeding wheels.

Alas!

Oh, everybody belongs to something,
But I don't belong to anything;
No, I don't belong to anything, any more than the
    miller of Dee,
And everything seems to belong
To people who belong to something,
But I don't belong to anything
So nothing belongs to me.

Racquet, Knickerbocker, Union League,
Shriners parading without fatigue,
Oddfellows, Red Men, Woodmen of the World,
Solvent Moose and Elks dew-pearled,
Tammany tigers, Temperance doves,
Groups of various hates and loves,
Success is the thing they all have an air of,
Theirs are the tickets that are taken care of,
Theirs are the incomes but not the taxes,
Theirs are the sharpest, best-ground axes;

Millions of members of millions of bands,
Greeting fellow members with helping hands;
Good fellows all in incorporated hordes,
Prosperity is what they are moving towards.

Alas!

Oh, everybody belongs to something,
But I don't belong to anything;
Yes, I belong to nothing at all, from Kiwanis to the
    R.F.C.,
And everything definitely belongs
To people who belong to lots of things,
But I don't belong to anything,
So nothing belongs to me.

THESE LATINS

The bashful Spaniardess apparently finds the amorous
    Spaniard so menacing to her virtue
That she has to employ a duenna so that he shan't duen-
    nacing to her virtue.

UP FROM THE WHEELBARROW

Some people understand all about machinery,

And to them it is just like beautiful poetry or beautiful scenery,

Because they know how to control and handle it,

Because they understandle it,

Yes, when they are confronted with a complicated piece of machinery,

Why, they are as cool and collected as a dean sitting in his deanery,

And I certainly wish I were among them because if there is one thing that makes me terrified and panical,

It is anything mechanical and nowadays everything is mechanical.

O thrice unhappy home

Whose master doesn't know the difference between a watt and an ohm!

O radio glum and silent as a glum and silent burial

When no one knows what to do about the grounding or the aerial!

O four-door sedan cantankerous and stubborn and Mad Hattery,

With none to give a thought to occasionally changing the oil or once in a while checking on the battery!

O telephone and vacuum cleaners and cameras and electric toasters and streamlined locomotives and artificial refrigeration,

O thermostats and elevators and cigarette-lighters and air-conditioning units and all ye other gadgets that make ours a mighty nation,

I think you are every one a miracle,

And you do wonderful things and it's probably only because I don't see how you do what you do that when I think of you I become hystirical,

And of course that is silly of me because what does it
  matter how you function so long as all I have to do to
  get you to function is push a button or throw a switch,
Always assuming that I can remember which is which,
So keep on functioning, please,
Because if you don't I shall starve or freeze.

NOTHING BUT NATURE

Ha ha ha! the sun is shining!
Yo ho ho! the sky is blue!
See the earth in peace reclining!
See the ocean reclining, too!
Tra la la! the birds are chirruping!
Fields are green and flowers are gay!
Maples swell with sap a-syruping!
Nature is spreading herself today!

Well, let's go out and trample on a violet,
Let's steal candy from a curly-headed tot,
Take a wrong number and deliberately dial it,
Let's plant thistles under squatters when they squat,
Let's throw pepper on the robins on their nests,
Let's tell Altman's we prefer to buy at Best's,
Let's cry Boo! at golfers as they putt,
Let's open windows that people want shut,
Let's step on somebody's nice white shoes,
Let's join a club and not pay dues,
Let's send bills and let's raise rents,
Let's put mosquitoes in campers' tents,
Let's teach Nature not to spread so free
On a day when my love is cross with me.

Yah yah yah! the rain is raining!
Zut alors! the wild waves boil!
Hear the homeless wind complaining!
Watch the shrubbery bite the soil!
Nya nya nya! come sleet, come icicles!
The world is a welter of freezing spray!
Pity the sailors on their high-wheeled bicycles!
Nature is having a tantrum today!

Well, let's buy lace from a visiting Armenian,
Let's give a beggar a nickel for a bath,
Let's praise Homer to a Homer-sick Athenian,
Let's spread sunbeams all along the path,
Let's go listen to the neighbourhood bores,
Let's help mothers through revolving doors,
Let's go to church and fill the plate with money,
Let's tell the minister the sermon was a honey,
Let's teach whales to avoid harpooners,
Let's be kind to congressmen and crooners,
Let's make hunters make friends with moose,
Let's buy songbirds and turn them loose,
And that will teach Nature to tantrum when
My love is speaking to me again.

One thing that literature would be greatly the better for
Would be a more restricted employment by authors of
simile and metaphor.
Authors of all races, be they Greeks, Romans, Teutons,
or Celts,
Can't seem just to say that anything is the thing it is but
have to go out of their way to say that it is like some-
thing else.
What does it mean when we are told
That the Assyrian came down like a wolf on the fold?
In the first place, George Gordon Byron had had enough
experience
To know that it probably wasn't just one Assyrian, it was
a lot of Assyrians.
However, as too many arguments are apt to induce
apoplexy and thus hinder longevity,
We'll let it pass as one Assyrian for the sake of brevity.
Now then, this particular Assyrian, the one whose cohorts were gleaming in purple and gold,
Just what does the poet mean when he says he came down
like a wolf on the fold?
In heaven and earth more than is dreamed of in our
philosophy there are a great many things,
But I don't imagine that among them there is a wolf
with purple and gold cohorts or purple and gold
anythings.
No, no, Lord Byron, before I'll believe that this Assyrian
was actually like a wolf I must have some kind of proof;
Did he run on all fours and did he have a hairy tail and a
big red mouth and big white teeth and did he say Woof
woof?
Frankly I think it very unlikely, and all you were entitled
to say, at the very most,
Was that the Assyrian cohorts came down like a lot of
Assyrian cohorts about to destroy the Hebrew host.

But that wasn't fancy enough for Lord Byron, oh dear me
no, he had to invent a lot of figures of speech and then
interpolate them,
With the result that whenever you mention Old Testament
soldiers to people they say Oh yes, they're the ones
that a lot of wolves dressed up in gold and purple ate
them.
That's the kind of thing that's being done all the time by
poets, from Homer to Tennyson;
They're always comparing ladies to lilies and veal to
venison,
And they always say things like that the snow is a white
blanket after a winter storm.
Oh it is, is it, all right then, you sleep under a six-inch
blanket of snow and I'll sleep under a half-inch blanket
of unpoetical blanket material and we'll see which one
keeps warm,
And after that maybe you'll begin to comprehend dimly
What I mean by too much metaphor and simile.

WATCHMAN, WHAT OF THE FIRST FIRST LADY?

Everybody can tell you the date of George Washington's birth,

But who knows the date on which Mrs George Washington first appeared on earth?

Isn't there any justice

For the former Mrs Custis?

Of course her memory is perpetuated in the name of an hotel,

But Hell.

It's a disgrace to every United State

That we don't know more about our first president's only mate.

We all know a lot of stories about the wife of King Arthur

But you never hear any about Martha.

And we have all read a lot of romantic tales about Catherine the Great,

But nobody even writes them about Washington's mate.

And we have all seen Katherine Cornell, or was it Helen Hayes or Ethel Barrymore,

Impersonate Cleopatra, who wasn't even anybody's real wife but nothing more or less than a promiscuous un-American parrymore,

But has anybody done anything about the mistress of the nation's whitest house?

No, and yet but for her the nation would be the child of a man without a spouse.

George Washington was a gentleman,
A soldier and a scholar;
He crossed the Delaware with a boat,
The Potomac, with a dollar.
The British faced him full of joy,
And departed full of sorrow;
George Washington was a gentleman.
His birthday is tomorrow.

When approached by fellow patriots,
And asked for his opinion,
He spoke in accents clear and bold,
And, probably, Virginian.
His winter home at Valley Forge
Was underheated, rather.
He possessed a sturdy Roman nose,
And became his country's father.

His army was a hungry horde,
Ill-armed, worse-clad Colonials;
He was our leading President,
And discouraged ceremonials.
His portrait on our postage stamps,
It does him less than justice;
He was much respected by his wife,
The former Mrs Custis.

He routed George's scarlet coats;
(Though oft by Congress hindered)
When they fortified the leeward side,
He slashed them from the windward.
He built and launched our Ship of State,
He brought it safe to harbour;
He wore no beard upon his chin,
Thanks to his faithful barber.

George Washington was a gentleman,
His birthday is tomorrow.
He filled his country's friends with joy,
His country's foes, with sorrow.
And so my dears, his grateful land
In robes of glory clad him.
George Washington was a gentleman.
I'm glad his parents had him.

WHERE THERE'S A WILL, THERE'S VELLEITY

Seated one day at the dictionary I was pretty weary and also pretty ill at ease,

Because a word I had always liked turned out not to be a word at all, and suddenly I found myself among the v's,

And suddenly among the v's I came across a new word which was a word called velleity,

So the new word I found was better than the old word I lost, for which I thank my tutelary deity,

Because velleity is a word which gives me great satisfaction,

Because do you know what it means, it means low degree of volition not promoting to action.

And I always knew I had something holding me back but I didn't know what,

And it's quite a relief to know it isn't a conspiracy, it's only velleity that I've got,

Because to be wonderful at everything has always been my ambition,

Yes indeed, I am simply teeming with volition,

So why I never was wonderful at anything was something I couldn't see

While all the time, of course, my volition was merely volition of a low degree,

Which is the kind of volition that you are better off without it,

Because it puts an idea in your head but doesn't prompt you to do anything about it.

So you think it would be nice to be a great pianist but why bother with practising for hours at the keyboard,

Or you would like to be the romantic captain of a romantic ship but can't find time to study navigation or charts of the ocean or the seaboard;

You want a lot of money but you are not prepared to work for it,

Or a book to read in bed but you do not care to go into the nocturnal cold and murk for it;

And now if you have any such symptoms you can identify
   your malady with accurate spontaneity:
It's velleity,
So don't forget to remember that you're velleitous, and if
   anybody says you're just lazy,
Why, they're crazy.

RIDING ON A RAILROAD TRAIN

Some people like to hitch and hike;
They are fond of highway travel;
Their nostrils toil through gas and oil,
They choke on dust and gravel.
Unless they stop for the traffic cop
Their road is a fine-or-jail road,
But wise old I go rocketing by;
I'm riding on the railroad.

I love to loll like a limp rag doll
In a peripatetic *salon*;
To think and think of a long cool drink
And cry to the porter, *allons*!
Now the clickety clack of wheel on track
Grows clickety clackety clicker:
The line is clear for the engineer
And it mounts to his head like liquor.

Oh give me steel from roof to wheel,
But a soft settee to sit on,
And a cavalcade of commerce and trade
And a drummer to turn the wit on.
Stuyvesant chats with Kelly and Katz,
The professor warms to the broker,
And life is good in the brotherhood
Of an air-conditioned smoker.

With a farewell scream of escaping steam
The boiler bows to the Diesel;
The Iron Horse has run its course
And we ride a chromium weasel;
We draw our power from the harnessed shower,
The lightning without the thunder,
But a train is a train and will so remain
While the rails glide glistening under.

Oh, some like trips in luxury ships,
And some in gasoline wagons,
And others swear by the upper air
And the wings of flying dragons.
Let each make haste to indulge his taste,
Be it beer, champagne, or cider;
My private joy, both man and boy,
Is being a railroad rider.

THE CAT

One gets a wife, one gets a house,
Eventually one gets a mouse.
One gets some words regarding mice,
One gets a kitty in a trice.
By two a.m., or thereabout,
The mouse is in, the cat is out.
It dawns upon one, in one's cot,
The mouse is still, the cat is not.
Instead of Pussy, says one's spouse,
One should have bought another mouse.

THIS WAS TOLD ME IN CONFIDENCE

Oh, I do like a little bit of gossip
In the course of a cosy little chat,
And I often wonder why
My neighbours all imply
I'm a pussy, I'm a tabby, I'm a cat.
Mrs Dooley murmured meow at me this morning;
Mrs Cohen would have cut me if she could;
But my feelings aren't so filmy
That names are going to kill me,
And a little bit of gossip does me good.

Oh, I do like a little bit of gossip;
I am pleased with Mr Moffet's double life.
It's provocative to watch
Mr Taylor guzzle Scotch;
I wonder if he knows about his wife?
The sheriff wants a word with Mrs Walker;
She doesn't pay her bills the way she should;
Yet I hear from several sources
That she gambles on the horses—
Oh, a little bit of gossip does me good.

Oh, I do like a little bit of gossip;
It seems to lend a savour to my tea;
The deplorable mistakes
That everybody makes
Are calories and vitamins to me.
If I tell you Mrs Drew is off to Reno,
You are not to breathe a word, that's understood;
For I said to Mrs Drew
That I heard it all from you—
Oh, a little bit of gossip does me good.

Oh, I do like a little bit of gossip,
But for scandal or for spite there's no excuse;
To think of Mrs Page
Telling lies about my age!
Well, her tongue is like her morals, rather loose.
Mrs Murgatroyd eats opium for breakfast,
And claims I'm running after Mr Wood;
That sort of vicious slander
Arouses all my dander—
But a little bit of gossip does me good.

THROUGH THE JUNGLE WITH PIKE AND STAFF

I

Abandon for a moment, friends,
Your frivolous means, your futile ends;
Life is not wholly beer and skittles,
A treasure hunt for love and victuals;
Nay, life is real, life is earnest,
Life is for ever doing its durnest;
And so at times I think we ought
To pause and think a sobering thought.
Myself, I feel a dark despair
When I consider human hair.
I'm chicken-hearted, beetle-browed,
As I behold the heedless crowd,
Knowing each carefree individual
The slave of hair that runs on schidual.
On every human head or chin
It's falling out or growing in.
Yon whistling adolescent scholar,
Released from Ye Olde Tonsorial Parlour,
Runs up his neck with fingers tense
Like sticks along a picket fence.
His scalp is all Bay Rum and bristles,
Therefore he's pleased and therefore whistles.
Yea, he rejoices, quite unknowing
That all the time his hair is growing.
O woe is you, unhappy scholar,
Next month you'll be back in the tonsorial parlour.

II

Myself I feel a dark despair,
When I consider human hair,
(Fine filaments sprouting from the skin),
I tremble like an aspirin.

For men and women everywhere
Unconsciously are growing hair,
Or, if the other hand you choose,
With every breath a hair they lose.
Unbid it cometh, likewise goeth,
And oftentimes it's doing boeth.
This habit is the chief determinant
Why permanent waves are less than permanent.
You rise, Madame, you face your mirror,
You utter cries of shame and terror.
What though to males you look all right?
For heaven's sake, you hair's a sight.
You hasten to the Gallic lair
Where lurks Maurice, or Jean or Pierre.
Between arrival and departure
You suffer hours of vicious torture,
At last emerging, white and weak,
But sure at least your name is chic.
Thus you rejoice, my dear, unknowing
That all the time your hair is growing.
The waves so dearly purchasèd,
Next month will have grown a foot or so away from your
    head.

III

I've said, I think, I think we ought
To think at times a sobering thought.
Man's lot it is to be a field
For crops that no nutrition yield,
That filter through his tender skin
And ripen on his head or chin.
I face mankind and shudder, knowing
That everybody's hair is growing;
That lovers, linked in darkened hallways,
Are capped with hair that groweth always;
That millions shaven in the morning,
At eve find beards their jowls adorning;

That hair is creeping through the scalps
Of yodellers yodelling in the Alps,
And pushing through the epidermises
Of peasants frolicking at kermises;
And poking bravely through the pores
Of cannibals on tropic shores;
That freezing, scorching, raining, snowing,
People's hair is always growing.
I contemplate with dark despair
The awful force of growing hair,
Although admitting, to be quite honest,
That it will be worth a million split atoms to humanity
    if Science can ever get it harnessed.

UNANSWERED BY REQUEST

There are several things in life that keep me guessing,

And one of them is what are the French words for French leave and French fried potatoes and French dressing,

And I am also a trifle vague

About how you ask people to a Dutch treat or talk to them like a Dutch uncle in The Hague.

And why do restaurants put signs in their windows advertising REAL HOME COOKING and expect the customers to come rushing in all panting and overjoyed

When the reason that half the people who eat in restaurants are eating in restaurants is because with home cooking they have become cloyed?

And when is a violin a fiddle?

And when the tide goes out here does it go in somewhere else or does it just pile up and make the ocean deeper in the middle?

And who is the brownie whose duty it is to see that the theatre curtain never goes up on time except the one evening that you are late?

And who is the railroad dispatcher who arranges his dispatching so that every time you are about to see something interesting out of your train window your view is cut off by a hundred-car freight?

All these moot questions and many others equally moot if not even mooter

Must be faced by every thinking male and female practically as soon as they graduate from their kiddiecar or scooter,

Because they are the kind of riddles and conundrums with which life

Is far too too rife,

But fortunately for the human race thinking people eventually discover that there is only one satisfactory way of dealing with a riddle or a conundrum.

And that is to stop worrying about the answers and just get clean out from undrum.

TO BE LET—UNFURNISHED

The Murrays are hunting a house,
They are tired of living in flats.
They long for a personal mouse,
And a couple of personal cats.
They are hunting a house to inhabit,
An Eden, or even an Arden,
They are thinking of keeping a rabbit,
They are thinking of digging a garden.
How giddy the Murrays have grown,
To aspire to a house of their own!

Oh, hurry, hurry!
Says Mrs Murray.
Tarry a while, says he.
If you care for a house
That is a house,
You'd better leave it to me.
I'd like an orchard, apple or pear,
I'd like some accessible bathing there,
And a den for plotting masculine plots,
And a lawn for practising mashie shots,
And open fires,
And a pleasant sun room,
A handy garage,
And perhaps a gun room,
And an atmosphere exempt of static,
And a heater silent and automatic.
For such a house
I would hurry, hurry—
I'm a practical man,
Says Mr Murray.

The Murrays of 17 B,
The Murrays are going away,
From the wireless in 17 C,
And the parties in 17 A.

For the Murrays are tired of flats,
They are rapidly growing aloof,
As they dream of their personal cats,
As they dream of their personal roof.
Their friends cannot smother their merriment
When they speak of the Murrays' experiment.

Oh, hurry, hurry!
Says Mr Murray.
Tarry a while, says she.
When we choose a house,
Let us choose a house
As nice as a house can be.
With a dozen windows South and East,
And a dozen capacious cupboards at least,
And a laundry lilting with light and air,
And a place for a wife to dry her hair,
And plenty of sun,
And plenty of shade,
And a neat little room
For a neat little maid,
And a wall with roses clambering wild,
And a quiet room for a sleepy child.
If you happen to see it,
Hurry, hurry!
For that's the house,
Says Mrs Murray.

UNDER THE FLOOR

Everybody knows how the waters come down at Lodore,
But what about voices coming up through the floor?
Oh yes, every time that into a task you set your teeth
Something starts talking in the room underneath,
And no matter how many authorities you quiz,
You can never find out who or what it is;
You know one thing about it and nothing more,
That it is just something that goes around making noises
    that come up through the floor,
And you never get a view of it,
But you deduce that there are at least two of it,
And sometimes it sings the Indian Love Call and some-
    times it sings Lead, Kindly Light, by Cardinal Newman,
But even then it doesn't sound human,
And sometimes it just gobbles,
And the sound wibbles and wobbles,
And sometimes it snarls like a ghoul interrupted at its
    unholy feast,
And sometimes it just mutters like blood going down the
    drain of a tub after a murderer has finished dismembering
    the deceased;
It cackles, it crackles, it drones, it buzzes, it chortles,
It utters words but in no tongue spoken by mortals,
Yes, its language is a mystery for evermore,
The language of whatever it is that makes the noise that
    comes up through the floor,
And you shiver and quiver and wonder,
What's under?
Is it banshees or goblins or leprechauns, or trolls or
    something?
Or pixies or vampires or lost souls or something?
What is it below?
Better not, better not know.

Don't let it upset you,
But also don't overlook the possibility that some day
whatever it is that makes the noises that come up
through the floor may come up through the floor and
get you.

WEDNESDAY MATINÉE

Oh, yes, I'd love to go to the play,
But not the Wednesday matinée.
I'd rather stay home with Lorna Doone
Than go of a Wednesday afternoon,
I'd rather work on a crumbling levee
Than cope with a Wednesday theatre bevy.
Women, women, and still more women;
A sea of drugstore perfume to swim in;
Tongues like sirens, and tongues like clappers,
And the ripping crackle of candy wrappers
(A fudge-nut sundae was all their lunch,
They are dying for something sweet to munch);
And foreheads grow moist and noses glisten,
It's everyone talk, and nobody listen;
Voice beats on voice, and higher and higher
Screams and steams the anarchic choir.
The early-comers sit on the aisle
With their laps in a Himalayan pile,
Every corpulent knee a sentry
Denying to all the right of entry.
The usher glances at laps and knees,
And murmurs, Show me your tickets, please.
The aborigines clatter and clack,
But they're next aisle over and eight rows back.
Thither they march, with candy and wraps,
To be balked by other knees and laps.
The house lights fade, the footlights glow,
The curtain rises. This is the show.
This is the charm, the enchanted flame,
That drew them here from wherever they came.
Over the house no silence falls,
But shopper to shopper desperate calls;
Suburban ladies their tonsils gird,
Determined to have one final word,

Interrupting their own ripe rush
To squelch their neighbours with cries of Hush!
The dialogue dies upon the stage
At the rustle and swish of the programme page.
With a wave of applause, terrific, tidal,
They recognize the star, their idol,
Undeterred by the sober fact
That she doesn't appear till the second act.
Now the whisper runs from row to row,
Doesn't the butler look like Joe?
And the mother's the image of Emily, kind of,
And who does the lover put you in mind of?
Now, like the drunkard scenting liquor,
The ladies sniff for dirt, and snicker;
Forgetting now their gum and fudge,
The ladies cackle and leer and nudge,
Rooting in every harmless line
For *double entendre* and obscene design;
Yet prompt with handkerchief and tears
The moment a child or a dog appears.
The curtain falls; the play is ended.
Adorable! Dreadful! Stupid! Splendid!
They cry of the play that was unattended,
Unheard, unseen, and uncomprehended.
O matinée maenads, O bulging bacchantes,
I would my pen were as sharp as Dante's,
But as it isn't I simply say
You may keep your Wednesday matinée.

REQUIEM

There was a young belle of old Natchez
Whose garments were always in patchez.
When comment arose
On the state of her clothes,
She drawled, When Ah itchez, Ah scratchez!

INDEX OF FIRST LINES